MBA

364.1532 HIL
Hill, Tori, author
I'm not the only

I'm Not The Only One

Tori Hill

364.1532
HIL

I'm Not the Only One
Copyright © 2019 by Tori Hill

All rights reserved. No part of this publication may be reproduced, distributed, or transmitted in any form or by any means, including photocopying, recording, or other electronic or mechanical methods, without the prior written permission of the author, except in the case of brief quotations embodied in critical reviews and certain other non-commercial uses permitted by copyright law.

Tellwell Talent
www.tellwell.ca

ISBN
978-0-2288-1922-6 (Hardcover)
978-0-2288-1920-2 (Paperback)
978-0-2288-1921-9 (eBook)

Dedication

To the survivors who are fighting. Fighting for the chance to be whole again. Fighting to understand why. Fighting to believe in trust and laughter and joy. Fighting for silence from their fears and nightmares.

Acknowledgments

*T*his book was inevitable. I just wasn't sure how or when I would get there. It has been a passion project and one that I hope serves its purpose. In getting here, it took a team of forces.

I want to thank my parents, my sisters and their families for their support over the years. Without it, I would never have gotten to this stage. Also, thank you for allowing me to include some of your experiences along with my story. While I am the one who was assaulted, this is something we all experienced, and I am grateful that I could show more than just one side.

Thank you to Mary and Ann who did the first couple of read throughs and gave me the confidence to continue down the path of publishing. Thank you to Alex who sat at the kitchen table with me and in the car on numerous occasions, discussing sections of my book. In many instances the three of you were the first run at identifying if I was on track.

A special thank you to Trina for taking the time to hear out my vision and take beautiful photographs for my cover. This was not an easy feat, and I am so appreciative that you spent the time to understand what I was attempting to create and the individuals I was hoping to help through the publishing of my story.

And finally thank you to everyone who helped me through the publishing and editing process of my story. Without you this would still just be words on a page, hidden from everyone's view.

Introduction

*I*t's hard for me to talk about what happened, even after all this time. I do my best to avoid it, especially in public spaces, but maybe its time to let that go. We are starting to hear more about sexual assault survivors, but in many cases the story ends at the rape. What happens after? Unless you have personally experienced the ups and downs after being assaulted or been part of the support system for a survivor, little is known.

As you can imagine, as a survivor of rape, the last thing I want to do is live in the past and keep reliving what happened. But the thing is – there is more to my story. I am still here; and my pain didn't end when the rape did. That was just the beginning of a tumultuous ride.

This isn't a happy or pretty story and it was difficult to write. I had to do this in stages, and in some cases force myself to write the words I've never wanted to fully admit.

I have always believed that someday I would write about my experience. I wasn't sure when that would happen or what it would look like. To me though, it was always important that when I was ready that I used my voice to help someone else. I want to bring an awareness that we seem to be missing or hesitant to accept.

The time came without warning.

I was driving home one day after a terrible week. Personally, and work-wise it hadn't been great. I was focused only on getting home to pick up my dog and then carrying on with my plans for the night. In my own world, not paying much attention I heard another announcement about a sexual assault. It caught me off-guard. It shouldn't have, but it did.

R. Kelly was once again in the news and accused of sexual assault. There have been many allegations against him over the years. I believe he is guilty; however, we are in the early stages, and he is still an "alleged" rapist. We will see what conclusion the courts come to but either way I feel for the victims. I know what it is like to be on their end. I hope for their sake they get the justice I never will. Coming forward is not easy. There is an internal battle that you go through first:

> Did this really happen? Am I about to ruin someone's life? What does this say about me? Am I now worthless? Am I weak? Is it worth it to say anything? What will other people think? What do I think? How do I feel? How…. The list goes on.

Acceptance is hard. Admitting to yourself that this really happened is awful. You fight it the whole way, waiting to wake up from this nightmare. Wondering how you could possibly have ended up here.

Maybe it hits me harder this time of year because the anniversary of my own experience is right around the corner. It seems like a lifetime ago now, but when I hear about things like this it all comes rushing back. The women who came forward in this story were young when they were attacked. Younger than I was. I think about how hard it was at 21 to deal with. I can't imagine having to process this as a teen, as a child.

We keep hearing about these experiences, and unfortunately, we will continue to. I don't pretend to have *the* answer. But at what point do we wake up?

I remember the voice of my attacker. Nine years later and I can still identify that voice. Nine years later and I still question why no one helped me.

The following pages are my story. For the sake of anonymity, I have changed the names. I hope that by reading this you understand a little more. I hope this is effective in explaining the significance of these issues. Rape isn't something that happens to one person, it happens to us all. I hope if you are someone that has experienced any type of sexual assault, that you understand that you are not the problem and that you are not alone.

And if you are reading this because someone you know was sexually assaulted, I hope this helps you understand the journey and challenges they are about the face. Try not to take their pain personally and get the support you need in order to best support them.

Chapter 1

Terror

I will never forget the moment it all started to click. The moment my denial of everything I was feeling started to break way. I was recovering from the worst hangover of my life. Not convinced that even then, I was completely sobered up. It was about 5pm when I finally started to feel like I could stand long enough to have a shower.

I didn't notice anything out of the ordinary as I got into the shower. I knew I was in pain, and had a ton of cuts and bruises all over my body. Honestly though, I couldn't remember anything from the night before, and while that was unusual, I just assumed I had fallen at some point. I wasn't really in a frame of mind where my logic was sound. Still fighting off the feeling that something wasn't right.

I am known for my ridiculously long showers. I love the water, and a hot shower is a wonderful feeling. I could stand there for hours. This day was different though. The water stung. The pressure felt stronger than usual and I had the urge to get out as quickly as possible.

As I turned off the shower and pushed back the curtain, I grabbed a towel to dry off before stepping out. The towel felt rough and I really didn't want it on me for longer than it needed to be. Our shower was right in front of a mirror, I used my towel to wipe away the fog that had built up and as I did my worst nightmare started to come true. When I saw my body now naked in front of the mirror I gasped and it all started to click. But even then, I wasn't ready to accept it just yet.

I am pretty fair, and I bruise somewhat easily…but not so easily that shapes of what caused the bruises can be seen. I literally had a bruise in the shape of his hand on my chest. As I looked closer, I could make out the bite marks around my nipples, bitten so hard they were scabbing over. (It's not easy to write that and is often a detail I skip over. It seems almost too personal and makes my stomach turn every time.) As I examined the rest of my body, I could see that there were bruises, bitemarks, cuts and scrapes all over.

When I see the details of what happened to me laid out in black and white it is so obvious…but when you are in denial it is really easy to convince yourself that you're seeing or feeling things that aren't accurate.

At this point, I still didn't want to accept it. These types of things aren't supposed to happen to girls like me. From what societal norms tell us, this happens in movies. It happens in areas that are unsafe or rougher communities. It happens when you are up to no good, or when you find yourself in a dark alleyway. It happens at gunpoint. This certainly doesn't happen in your own home, and if it did, wouldn't you remember? How can you forget something so terrible? How could you have let someone into your home? No, it mustn't be true. There is no possible way.

I'm Not the Only One

As all of these thoughts were fighting for attention, I was trying as hard as possible to forget. I was not ready to accept this or even think about it. I didn't cry, I didn't say anything to my roommates. I didn't say anything to my friends. I continued on with my day as if it was just a normal hangover.

I had plans that night with, one of my best friends, Alex. Her and I had been in school together since junior high, had become friends in high school and then ended up at the same university. We were in different programs and with me also being on a school team, our schedules mostly conflicted. It had taken a month to find a date that worked for both of us, so even though by this time I knew something was wrong, I just wanted a distraction. I continued on with our plans, not letting on that anything was out of the ordinary. When Alex got to my place, her and I walked to get ice cream. I was pretty quiet that night, which for anyone who knows me well was unusual. I didn't say anything about how I was feeling, trying to push my thoughts away.

On the way back, I let what was in my head finally spill out. I was still keeping it together. Everything was factual. Alex was a pre-med student at the time and asked me questions that made me think. She was calm and collected and let me come to terms with it on my own. When I did, it was just a wave of tears. I couldn't control it, I couldn't breathe and I didn't know what to do. All I wanted was to get away. I didn't know where "away" was, but I wanted to be there.

She talked me through what I needed to do next. Not pushing me to do anything, more just letting me rationalize and make a plan. She stayed with me for a bit, and then eventually I sent her home.

I saw Alex a month or so ago, she was home visiting and we went out for dinner with another friend of ours. Somehow, we go onto the topic of what had happened back then. While the event happened to me, Alex is also haunted by that day. We talked about how she knew something wasn't right, but she couldn't put her finger on it. Alex is so sincere and when she talks about it, you can hear the pain in her voice. Even now, it is just as raw to her as it is to me.

Alex admits that some of the finer details of that night are difficult to remember. She remembers that I seemed confused and in disbelief. She told me how I kept repeating, "I think there was a guy in my house. I think there was a guy in my room but I don't remember." She said she was in such disbelief, not at what I was saying, but that it could happen. She talks about how as I was telling her, she just wanted to make sure that I was OK. Like me, she was stuck on how this isn't supposed to happen to people we know. She remembers that when I showed her my chest and the bruising, it started to sink in for her how serious the situation really was. As this was happening, I just kept repeating, "I think there was a guy in my room," as if trying to convince myself that it was just a bad dream and that at anytime, I would wake up.

Alex went into protection mode. Trying to think of anything and everything I needed to do. She did her best to help me digest what had happened and identify the next steps. I had showered, it had been 24 hours. Already so much crucial evidence was gone, but when you aren't aware of what happened you don't know what the correct steps are. As the saying goes, *we don't know what we don't know.*

While her and I don't often talk about what happened, that discussion was important. That event solidified so much of our friendship. Knowing that in the worst moment of my life she could be there for me, has brought an unbreakable trust. This year, it has been my turn to console her through some dark times, and times of loss. While the events are unfortunate and sad, I am happy to have her in my life and to be able to offer her a shoulder to cry on. It is the least I can do, after everything she has done for me.

Chapter 2

The Night Before

It was a night of celebration—the athletic banquet. A night to recognize all of the university teams. It had been another successful season at my university. My team won our conference yet again and placed in the top 10 at Nationals. The bigger win for me was that I finally broke through my mental block. That was a big deal…you have no idea. After a couple of significant injuries throughout my university years, I was unable to train the way I had in the past. As a result, I found it hard to adjust my expectations. I still wanted to be the best in my event, but the reality was my body was no longer able to do that. I never felt that I was doing enough, that I was competing the right way or that I was good enough. That year I finally let myself just enjoy the sport again. The adrenaline of competing. I let myself have fun. It wasn't about the result, it was about just being in the moment. And for the first time in 4 years, I didn't feel like I let everyone down. It was the first time I had seen improvement since high school, so it was time to also let myself enjoy that. The little wins.

The athletic banquet had always been a big night. It was the one night we had to recognize the successes of those on other sports teams. As per other years, we would rush back from class and meet up with friends. We would have a couple drinks as we were getting ready for the evening. Three of us had made jello shots for the group that was getting ready together.

We would then meet up with the rest of the team, have a few more drinks during reception, and a few more with dinner. We were trying to behave in front of the faculty and coaches, of course. Take a break through awards, then the after-party. I don't pretend alcohol wasn't involved, but alcohol isn't to blame. Drinking doesn't equate to consent. Alcohol cannot provide consent. That seems to be a fact that gets conveniently forgotten.

The after-party was at a local bar. While in other years we had a private event, this year it was open. Athletes who were of legal age had tickets and were on the VIP list, but anyone could get into the bar.

The Sexual Assault Team that was brought in for me told me that this particular bar (as well as a few others in town) had a scheme going on. It worked like this: one person would be inside slipping drugs into unsuspecting individuals' drinks, while the other was outside waiting for the perfect opportunity. This night, my number was up.

I can tell you exactly when it happened. I was at the bar with my friend and teammate, Sarah. I ordered a drink and she ordered a shot. I turned away from my drink (still in my hand) for 1 second as she took her shot. And that was it.

I'm Not the Only One

Now, society would tell you I did the wrong thing. While I was holding onto my glass, I was not laser focused on it at all times. I left myself susceptible. Some would say this makes it my fault.

From what I have been told, and have since had flashbacks that support, it wasn't long until things started to go wrong. I heard I was different and something seemed off from how I usually was when having consumed a few too many. In the discussions, days after, my teammates told me it was like I lost control of my body. That I was struggling to get my legs to work. They said that, looking back, they should have known something was wrong. They had never seen me in a state where my mind and body seemed to be working against each other. In their reflection they said it should have been obvious that there was something more than a bit too much alcohol. But hindsight is 20/20, and no one was their best self.

From the accounts of others, at one point I went to the washroom and I never came back.

Chapter 3

Drugged, Drunk and Alone

I began getting flashbacks a couple of days later. They were out of order and materialized over a matter of weeks. From what I have put together, I was kicked out of the bar. The security tapes confirm that. I also have flashbacks of myself asking the bouncers to find one of my roommates. The instance of a discussion is supported by the security video, but of course there is no sound.

What is interesting and infuriating, is that you can clearly tell there is something wrong and no one stepped up to do anything. The bouncers left a young girl (I guess adult is the right word) on the street, incapacitated and alone. In the security video it is very clear that something is wrong. The bouncers should have known, they are trained for this. It is strange that they left me alone outside the bar. Anytime I have ever seen someone removed from a bar, the bouncers always had a friend with the individual. I question why they didn't do this for me. Why did they not escort me to find a friend? Why was I ignored? I will never know.

In my university town, the police would pull people off the street and put them in what we called the drunk tank until morning. No charges were laid, it was a safety measure the city had in place. The biggest thing they would do is take your shoelaces so you couldn't hurt yourself or others. In the morning when you had sobered up, they would release you. I wish that had been done for me. Instead I was left to fend for myself, drugged, drunk and alone. And then it gets worse...

Shortly after speaking with the bouncer, an individual comes up to me. The security video that follows was horrific to watch and has made me physically ill on more than one occasion. I have watched the first part of my assault. At this point it was physical. I can see myself being pinned up against the brick wall, the cuts and bruises all down my back would suggest this wasn't gentle. I was not alone in a dark alley, the wall I was pinned up against was not far from the entrance of the bar. There were many people on the street, and no one did a thing.

You can see that I manage to free myself, and eventually get into a cab. You can also see him follow me. Interestingly enough, no cab company would admit to providing a ride to my address that night. They all insisted that it was an out-of-town cab company. It's bullshit, but I cannot prove it. The security footage showed me getting into a cab, but you cannot tell which cab company it is. However, a cab *did* drive to my house that night.

Every once in awhile I remember split seconds of being in the cab. No particular details, just that I was in it. I can't tell you any details about the driver. I can't even tell you if the driver was male or female, just that I was in a cab. I get out of the cab and walk up to my door, and with that my nightmare continues but I can't comment much on what happened.

I now know I was strangled. Given that I have no memory of the actual rape, I assume I was strangled to the point of unconsciousness. I don't know at what point my body was roughed up. I can't tell you if it was before or while I was unconscious. My mind has refused to remember any of that time period, flashbacks kick back in after… always out of body.

The first flashback that would come back to me is mostly of his voice. For the longest time I couldn't get his Cape Breton accent out of my mind. It was like it was stuck on repeat. The way he would enunciate certain words haunted my thoughts. My only memory of him speaking to me is after. It comes to light halfway through a sentence, almost as if I am coming out of sedation. Nothing positive is said. He called me all kinds of things. Things I would never call another individual. It's hard to think about where my mind was during this. At times, I can have a temper and get pretty upset, but that's not my demeanour. I didn't react in anger, or rush to do much. My instinct was that I was still in danger and I needed to keep him calm. I remember letting him say these awful things and just begging him to leave.

The act of begging someone is one that makes you feel weak. It takes all of your power away. The idea of begging someone to stop doing things you do not want is degrading. There is no sunny side to that situation. It is not something I ever imagined having to do in my life. I grew up in Canada, this doesn't happen here. That's not what I had been led believe. We are supposed to live in a country that values the lives of all. That has equality. But it's a charade. I had seen and experienced inequality in my life, but never to this extent. I did not believe up until this point that feminism was something we needed. I will admit, I always thought it was for women who liked to complain. For individuals who were just never going to be happy. My eyes have been opened. I now believe feminism is vital until no woman has to beg for her safety and full control over her body. More people need to get on board and push for drastic changes.

When I go back to my memory of begging him leave, I can see him a blurred version of him, not any details, sitting in my computer chair. Sitting there and staring at me. Almost like he was proud of what had just happened. He's angry though, if that makes sense. Angry at me, insulted that I am in tears and just trying to convince him to leave. Eventually he agrees. And then its over. It's finally over.

I must have followed him downstairs when he left because our front door was locked the next morning. No one heard me, and I don't remember. I asked the nurses how it was possible that I could not remember someone being with me or locking the door after he left. They told me the drugs put you into a state where your body goes through the regular routines and motions without your awareness; almost like you're on autopilot.

Chapter 4

The Facts

Before we delve in any further, we need to cover some facts about rape. Most importantly: it is a fact that rape exists and happens. If you cannot accept that simple fact, there is really no reason for you to continue reading. We will never agree, and you will never understand that we need a solution. Fast.

A woman cannot "ask" for rape. This is an infuriating oxymoron. If we say women are "asking" for it, then what we are really saying is that women are an inferior gender and their appearance and sex organs mean that if they say "no" to the sexual wants of another individual then they *deserve* what comes to them. What you are really saying is that a woman's duty is to be a "yes" woman. If she says no, then what comes to her is her fault. This is still not "asking for it" – you cannot ask to be raped. You can ask for sex; you cannot ask for rape. There is no middle ground or leeway here. It is one or the other.

How an individual dresses, how much they drink or where they go does not provide consent. We hear it over and over again. This narrative needs to change.

"Look what she was wearing. Of course, she was raped. How did she not see that coming?"

The last time I checked, your clothes do not have the ability to provide consent. It is sexist and misogynistic to tell women that if what they wear is deemed sexual or risqué, then rape is an appropriate reaction for a man to have. As females we should have the same rights as males and be able to wear what we are comfortable in. You either believe in equality and freedom of choice, or you don't.

"She had so much to drink, what did she expect to happen?"

As a favourite meme of mine put it: she expected a hangover. That is what she expected to happen.

Rape is not "God's will." Sorry George Frought, but NO. This pisses me off to no end. If you are going to follow everything the Bible says to the T, then there are a lot of things that we need to change. Also, if you think that "God" believes in rape and wants it to happen, why do you follow this "God"? There are so many forms of religion in the world, why pick one that supports and enforces evil acts on humanity? If we are saying that this is His will, then are we also blaming racism, poverty, cancer, genocide, murder and war on Him, too? Where does it end? At some point, humanity needs to take responsibility for their actions. You cannot hide behind religion to save your backwards views on the world.

I'm Not the Only One

A few follow-up questions for you, Mr. Fraught. If Rape is "God's will" what about the following:

- *Is it only God's will if the rape involves a man and a woman? What happens when rape is man on man? Involves a transgender or non-binary individual? Is woman on woman? Or the woman rapes a man? Still "God's will"?*

- *If we are relying only on "God's will" then why is fertility treatment legal? If "God" wanted you and your partner to have a child, surely, he would allow you get pregnant naturally. Why are we tampering with "God's will"?*

- *Same question, but for adoption. Why is adoption legal? If we are relying on "God's will" then only those deemed by "God" as worthy of having children should be able to get pregnant. As a result, only those who have a natural birth should be allowed to be parents. If "God" has not given you that gift, and willed life on you, then you should not be deemed fit to be a parent.*

- *How about Viagra? If "God" wanted you to procreate, surely, he would allow you to have an erection. If you can't, then we should not be stepping in the way of "God's Will."*

For clarification I strongly disagree with all statements above. I think the notion of using "God" to push through policies should be disallowed. Why have we not yet learned that, even within religion, not everyone prays to the same "God." Who gets to decide which "God" is the true God? And for those individuals leftover, with a belief in no God, or whom are more spiritual in nature, why is your view more correct?

"Most rape is consensual anyway."

Barry Hovis supported the Missouri ban on abortion, which has no exceptions for rape by stating that "most rape is consensual anyway." In the same way that no one "asks" for rape, there is no such thing as consensual rape! Rape is when someone forces themselves on you. No person can consent to rape. If you consent, it is no longer someone unwantingly penetrating you, or you being forced to unwillingly penetrate someone. Consensual rape is a contradictory statement. If you believe that the "rape" was consensual, then you believe there was no rape at all. Instead you believe that this was a sexual act and not one of power. You believe that the victim is a liar, a slut or a whore, or some combination of all three. You do not respect the boundaries of the individual. Some would say you are the problem. Let's be clear: I'm saying that. I am calling you out. You are the problem.

"Sexual assault is rare and I do not know anyone it has happened to."

False! Sexual assault is grossly underreported, but that does not make it rare. In North America, 1 in every 4 women will be sexually assaulted.[1] Given that statistic there is a very good chance someone you know has been sexually assaulted. That does not mean that they have shared that personal information with you, nor do they need to. Not every sexual assault goes as far as rape, but that does not make it any less serious of an issue.

"Sexual assaults are commonly falsely reported."

Incorrect! There is always going to be someone who lies. There is no way around this, but the statistics in Canada for falsely reported sexual assaults is between 2-4%.[2] This is one of the only instances where that small percentage of liars has been used against victims to group *ALL* as liars. That shows how deep this issue really goes.

People lie about being robbed, but we do not say that everyone who reports a robbery is a liar. Since accusations of rape are predominately viewed as an attack on men, society has twisted the facts and blames the victim. The accused simply says the victim is looking for revenge, and his word is all they need. They believe his word, without any further evidence.

The last thing that we need to understand is that rape is not about sex, it is about control. When an individual does not listen to what the other party is telling them, he/she/they are exerting his/her/their control over them. This individual is expressing that the other party's boundaries and safety are meaningless. That the only thing that matters is what this individual — the one deemed superior — wants.

Now that we are on the same page, let's continue.

Chapter 5

Putting Things Together

A day or two after the initial flashbacks, another one appeared. I see everything as a third party, from the view of my closet. I can see that it is me on my bed, and he is on top of me, but somehow my mind has disassociated itself from the event. I am watching myself.

I don't understand how drugs can trick our brains into removing ourselves from the situation to make it look like you are someone else who is watching. Your brain does not allow you to know how you felt in that moment. I am so grateful for this. It was hard enough to keep living this life with what I do remember, I don't know that I would be here today if I remembered it differently. It feels wrong to say that…I am happy I was drugged? It's weird, right? I would be happier if I hadn't been drugged AND had been safe that night, but that was not meant to be.

How do I know that I was, in fact, raped that night? Let's just say I experienced a sneak peak of what new moms go through after giving birth. My body was ripped and it didn't heal overnight. I feel like my body initially went into shock and hid the pain from me. It wasn't until I had no choice but to accept what happened that the pain from the trauma kicked in.

Unfortunately, your body remembers trauma, even when your mind does not. My body tore and went through a lot of pain that night. While that healed years ago, my body now tears very easily. I try not to think too much about it, but in the back of my mind I always know why.

It took me a long time to put the memories in order, and even now it is still difficult. You hear it when I talk about the event. My thoughts bounce around out of order. Discussing one part of the event triggers a memory of something that happened before — something I have not explained to the listener. I go back to that, which leads to something else and very quickly my thought process goes off into a new direction. It can be difficult to follow for the listener. But it's real.

The first twelve hours after, I had no idea anything had even happened. My first memory (not flashback) of the next day is coming downstairs mid-afternoon to my roommate, Eric, asking me if I felt better. I looked at him funny, and asked what he meant. He said I had been in pretty rough shape when we were chatting earlier. Of course, I had no idea what he was talking about. I was tired and annoyed. I assumed he was just trying to get a rise out of me and asked him what he meant. It turns out he had come into the kitchen that morning and I was sitting there by myself in a trance. He said it was bizarre. Firstly, where I was sitting was unusual for me. Eric had this terrible computer chair that he replaced during the year. Instead of getting rid of it he put it beside the mini freezer. He knew how much I hated it being there and it didn't make sense that it was there. We had a kitchen table and chairs.

Anyway, there I was, sitting in the stupid, broken, computer chair. Apparently, we had a conversation, but he said at first, he couldn't even get me to respond and when I finally did it was like I was somewhere else. Having known me for a few years, he thought it was odd, but then again sometimes I am a little odd.

I had the worst hangover of my life that day. I had never had a headache. I miss those days. I was the person whose body would punish me if I overdid it by waking up insanely early. I would be up by 6:00 a.m. the next morning. I could also get up for a bit, have a stomach ache, and then go back to bed by 8:00 a.m. and be fine (just grumpy) when I woke up later. I was rarely sick. I learned early on to stay away from certain types of alcohol and most of the time knew when to cut myself off. The next day was not like that at all! I was so incredibly sick, and so sore into the evening. I couldn't eat for most of the day, I couldn't sleep, I couldn't really move. I had never experienced anything like that before and haven't since.

Chapter 6

The Phone Call

After my walk and conversation with Alex, I knew I had to make the worst phone call of my life. Calling your family to tell them what happened is not something you ever imagine doing. But at this point, all I knew was I needed some help and I didn't want to be out East. I remember just calling and saying that something happened and asking my mom not to be mad. At 21, the last thing I wanted was a bail out from my parents. I was becoming independent. I was figuring out what it means to be an adult and excited for what that looked like. All of that was gone in an instant. I wanted to shrink and just hide in a corner where no one could see me. I wanted to wake up from this awful nightmare and continue growing.

After the call, everything is a blur. My parents took action, there was no more thinking needed by me. My mom called me back a few minutes later and told me a female police officer would be coming over. While she was trying to be strong for me, I could hear the fear and pain in her voice.

One of my roommates had some friends over and I let them know it might be best to leave. At this point, it was unfortunately a reality and one of the girls asked a few stereotypical questions:

Girl: "What were you wearing?"

Me: "A semi-formal dress. It was an athletic banquet."

Girl: "Well how much did you drink?"

Me: "Does it matter?"

Girl: "Are you sure you just didn't make a mistake and regret it today?"

Eric jumps in: "She doesn't make mistakes."

I was very happy to not have to answer that last question. You would think that we would learn that this is not the appropriate form of questioning. I don't know you and you are in my house. How about we try "Are you OK?" or "What can I do?" or even "Oh my god, I am so sorry" if you have no other words.

A few minutes later the female police officer arrived and it was official: this was real. The officer asked me a few questions, and looked around the house. I find it weird that she didn't take anything from my room. In her questioning she asked me if I was going to be pressing charges. At this point, I was still grappling with what happened, I hadn't even thought about that. I said I didn't know. So, she did nothing, and took no evidence from my room. Instead she let me know she was taking me to the hospital and what to bring with me. I was a robot at this point, just going through the motions and following directions.

I'm Not the Only One

Have you ever been in a police car? The front doesn't seem so bad, but the back is awful. The seats of this cruiser were made of hard plastic. The doors don't open from the inside. As if I didn't have enough emotions going on, I felt like a criminal. I don't remember why, but she had a reason for me having to be in the back. I never want to be there again.

When you go into the hospital as a sexual assault victim, triage is different. While I believe I still had to provide everything, my name was entered anonymously into their system. I did not wait in the normal waiting area. I was taken to a private area, Eric and the police officer in tow. As I waited, I was asked all kinds of questions. I think I was still in shock.

After the officer was done with her questions, she sat with me and waited. Eric stayed for bit before being sent home. We were waiting for the Sexual Assault Team to arrive. They had been called in, but no one seemed to live close by. I still find it strange that there was no one on site that could have done something. Seems rather ridiculous to me actually.

It felt like we waited for hours. When they finally arrived, they took my clothes from the night before, completed my rape kit, asked me a lot of questions, looked me over, took photos and measured the bruises that had come out throughout the day. They took my blood for HIV testing and also administered some basic medications to make sure I didn't have to worry about the common STIs. One of the nurses even asked me if I wanted my dress back.

"Do you want your dress back?" one of the nurses asked.

"No."

"But it's so pretty," she said.

Tearing up, I said, "I am never going to wear it again. I don't even want to see it."

"I guess that makes sense, it's a shame though," she said. "It is cute."

"...."

It was during my examination when the team of nurses told me about the set-up going on downtown. They had heard it a few times, but weren't having any luck getting word to the public. They also told me that while the drug test wasn't showing strong enough evidence, everything I was feeling and how I had described my night led them to believe I was drugged with Ketamine. They indicated this was not the first time they had seen this drug being used in these events and that my lack of memories and the flashbacks were consistent with Ketamine. I am pretty naïve when it comes to drugs, so I really have no idea. They, however, were confident, but said the downside of it is that it leaves your system very quickly.

The nurses also told me that I could expect more memories to come back over the next few weeks. That I should not be surprised if I had more flashbacks and that they may include the actual rape. They tried to prepare me, but hearing and experiencing are not the same.

I was given a pamphlet that summarized everything they did and what I was treated for. I still have it. For some reason I haven't been able to part with it. It is hidden away, so someone won't fall upon it, but I know where it is.

After everything was complete, I was taken back to my place. Eric had gone home a couple hours earlier but was still up with my other roommates when I got back. The officer drove me. I didn't sleep much that night. I cried a lot.

Chapter 7

The Following Weeks

My parents flew out the next day. They didn't book a return ticket or a hotel. They didn't bring luggage. They were waiting to see me and let me make a decision. They took one look at me and already knew before they asked. I just wanted to be home. They packed some of my things and flew me home that night. I am lucky to have a supportive family. I don't know where I'd be without them. Not everyone has that, but I am happy that I do.

The line to a lot of people was that I had to move home for a family emergency. I don't generally disclose that *I* was the emergency.

The first night home was the hardest. I was in my childhood room, a place that had always been safe. But now it didn't feel that way. Everything was the same as I had left it, but it was different somehow. I was so, so tired, but I couldn't sleep. I felt afraid to be alone. I remember contemplating calling my sister, and asking her to come stay with me. That seemed rather silly when my parents were across the hall. I talked myself out of it, convincing myself she would think I was being overly dramatic. Instead I was alone with my thoughts and tears. That was not a fun place to be.

A lot of things went through my head that night, things I have never told anyone. I thought about what would happen if I ended up pregnant. I was on birth control and knew this was extremely unlikely, but I am a person who plays a lot of "what if?" scenarios in my mind. Due to where I was in my cycle, the hospital hadn't provided me with the morning after pill and there was always the off-chance that something could happen. I knew if it did, that I would have to make a choice. While I knew I would not be able to care for this fictional child on my own, my thoughts drifted into what would happen. I thought about the different options. For me abortion would not have been an option. I am pro-choice, but abortion is not for me. I would never have been able to forgive myself, but having to go through that thought process makes me understand how others could choose it.

Adoption was an alternative, but I would be concerned that the fictional child would be worse off with someone else. So, then I decided that if this was what the future had in store for me, that I would ask a family member to either adopt or take temporary custody while I figured things out and pulled myself back together. My biggest fear in all of this was what if the child looked like him and not me. That might just be too much and I wasn't convinced I would ever be able to look at this child as my own or truly accept them. "What if?" scenarios can lead you down quite the rabbit hole. Strange topic to go through, but the night is long.

I thought for a long time if I even wanted to continue being here. How could I make not being here easier on my family? What could I possibly say to them? Would they forgive me? Where would I leave my letter? How could I leave this life without causing them more pain? I wondered if they would understand, if they would be angry, or if not being here and all of this ending would just be a relief. Not the best thoughts to have, ones I no longer do, but those were in the forefront of my mind for the initial period of time. When you are in that amount of shock and pain, it is hard not to let your thoughts go there. It is even more difficult to not give in.

That wasn't the end though because exams were a week away. The school had permission to discuss school-related issues and decisions with my parents. I found out later I had the option to delay my exams but my parents didn't let me know that. I could not have handled that. My parents were right to not have me delay them. I can't say I studied overly hard that semester. I cared about my grades, but I just wanted it to be over, whatever the result.

I had special permission to write my exams at the local university in my hometown. While I didn't know that I could have delayed writing them completely, we did have a conversation on how I could choose which days to write. I chose to write on the same days and at the same times as I would have if I was at school.

One of my profs, the one who actually sat me down and told me I needed—yes, needed—to become an accountant, was fantastic throughout this ordeal. She took the reins and got a hold of all of my professors and sorted out everything for me the best she could. She would call every couple of days to see how things were going. I needed her in my corner.

There was one professor that was a problem. He thought I had lied and made up an excuse to get special treatment. He did not believe there was an emergency and he did not send my exam. He was prepared to fail me. It was a whole thing…he lost. My exam was eventually sent, an hour late. He later tried to fail me in terms of my participation mark, which was 10% of my grade for the class. That was also quickly corrected when I escalated the issue to the academic advisor. Some people are just assholes. As if victims of rape do not have enough going on, we then also have to deal with individuals who try to take advantage of their positions of power.

I failed a final exam for the first time that semester (my prof swears I got a B…ya I was there, I didn't), but I didn't care. I am pretty sure I was close to failing multiple exams that semester, but no professor would actually admit that (I can think of one who likely tried though). I did finish with a C in that professor's class. It is the worst grade on my entire transcript by a long shot. For my other courses, my grades dropped significantly, but from A/A+ to B+/A-. Not anything I was going to get overly worked up about. I was satisfied to be done.

I wrote one exam, and then had to go straight to the police station to give my verbal statement. I am not sure if I had to do it again because the police in my hometown were working with the police out East. I just know that was something I was required to do. I cried to myself throughout the entire exam. I'm sure other students thought I was breaking under the stress of exams. I tried my best to be quiet as I cried, but I am not convinced that I was overly successful.

Being at the police station was a different process, too. Since my dad was once an officer there, and some of the officers that he worked with were still active in the department, I was moved into a private office while I waited. This was done in case anyone recognized me. It was a way to keep gossip from stirring and allow me to maintain my anonymity. I sat by myself until the officer in charge of my case was ready for me. He also knew my dad, his brother and my dad worked closely together, and he had started with the force a few years before my dad left.

As if that wasn't enough, I wrote my last exam, to then leave immediately from it for the airport to have to deal with my stuff out East. It sucked, but I did it.

In between all of this, I would just burst into tears. Nothing in particular would happen, I would just cry. I couldn't control it. I just had to let it happen. It could be mid-sentence and — BAM — storm of tears. I could just be standing there, and then they'd come. It could be after laughter or just when sitting with family not saying anything. No warning, just a flood of tears.

I began to have a hard time with some of the language we use. I found it too difficult to use the word "rape" and I definitely didn't like the connotation of the word "victim." I started only referring to my attack as a sexual assault and to myself as a survivor. Today I find that I switch back and forth in the verbiage I choose. It often depends on the situation and the context. There are times when I find that using "rape" is more effective than "sexual assault" and vice versa. There are also times when I use the word "victim." My perspective on this word has changed though. Being referred to as a "victim" is not necessarily weak. It can hit home with people in a different way than "survivor." Don't get me wrong, I am still a survivor and know that I have come a long way. The thing is, the audience occasionally needs to be reminded that yes, I am a strong person, and I did overcome this, BUT the situation was forced on me. At times, the audience needs to be reminded how severe these events are, and I find changing up my choice of words is more impactful on them. It is no longer just about my needs, but also what others need to hear to feel the significance.

Chapter 8

A Mother's Perspective

When I started writing this book, I didn't tell anyone about it. Then I told a couple of friends, and once I got as far as deciding this wasn't just for me, I informed my immediate family. In doing so, I knew I was going to bring up a lot of pain. Things we have all acknowledged and tried to move on from.

I wrote my family an email:

> Hi,
>
> I thought you should all be aware that I am writing a book about my experience. I have known for 5 or 6 years that I would eventually do this. I have started to write it more than once, but this time it is becoming something.
>
> I am self-publishing, which means I have full control of the story and

cannot be told what I can and cannot include.

It maybe isn't the best time given how busy everyone is, but I didn't choose that, it sort of chose me if that makes sense. When I started to write it down, it was initially just for me. I couldn't get it out of my head one day. That version is long gone by now. That one was just a ramble of thoughts and not in any particular order.

The purpose is really for awareness and to show that it isn't just one person that is impacted. The idea is also to bring attention to how as a society we stop at the event, but do not consider the ripple effect and the how that can shape the rest of one's life.

My preference would actually be that none of you ever read it, as there is a lot in there that you do not know, but that is up to you. It is raw and dark, but it is real.

You can talk to me about it, but it is a bit easier to tell everyone at once through an email and gives you time to absorb it as well.

Tori

I have a pretty good relationship with my mom. Like all parents, there are moments where she drives me crazy. I am sure there are more times that I drive her mad. Her and I have had the most conversations about my assault. She was the one I called. She was the one who heard it in my voice before I could make out the words.

In our discussions she expressed how having your child assaulted is a parent's worst fear come true. That as a parent all you want is for your child to be safe.

One of the nights we were talking about my assault I went back to my memory of the sexual assault unit at the hospital. When I moved home, one of the first things my mom did was find out where I would go here for check-ups and testing. Since I was switching hospitals and the nurse who would be treating me had not yet seen me, I was asked to come in that week.

We sat in this large room that doubled as her office and also had a private examination table, separated by a curtain. First, we talked and then I was asked to change so she could examine me.

The file from my initial rape kit and photos had been sent to her. As she was examining me, she noticed that additional bruising had come out over the last few days. She took additional photos, and once again measured the bruises, noting the measurements in her chart. As she was completing her examination, she noticed the lacerations around my neck. This was the first time they had been mentioned to me and she was very concerned about them. We had a discussion about how I needed to monitor my breathing over the next week and if there was ANY indication of trouble breathing, I was to go to the ER right away.

During this examination I always thought my mom was on the other side of the curtain. I did not realize that when I changed, she was escorted to another room and not allowed back in until the exam was over.

As we were recounting the early events, I casually mentioned how awful that moment was, thinking that she had lived it too. I thought we just did not speak of it because of my sisters. In that moment the severity of my assault sunk in for both of us. My mom had always known how battered I was, but she did not know that it could have been worse. Having to break that news to her caught us both off-guard. Here I thought we had both processed that fact; I did not know that she did not hear the concern in the nurse's voice. It was like breaking the news of my assault to my mom all over again.

From there it led to a conversation about how bad it could have been. My mom just kept repeating that she was going to be sick. That she could have lost me. I had nine years to process that part of my assault, and she had only moments.

We have talked about other parts of the assault and days after. We have talked about not being taken seriously and issues with the school. I lived just off campus and there had already been issues in the area of a known male who would sneak into houses and hide out all day. Women would then wake up in the middle of the night with him watching them sleep. It was a creepy story and one that students were made aware of and reminded to keep their doors locked.

The school had security and they were supposed to be the ones that relayed this type of information to those in charge. They were the ones who were supposed to help get information out to students. My assault was part of a sick, planned out process at the local bars. It was a game played by the assailants. And yet, the individual at security my mom informed of the incident and explained the scheme to laughed at her, and stated that she could try calling back later, he was

I'm Not the Only One

going to get his lunch. He was not willing to relay this information to his supervisor or anyone else. Not when he had a belly that was getting empty. I think that is sick. That also sums up everything that activists of sexual assault awareness have been trying to say. It sums up the feelings that the SANE nurses had about the event. They knew about the scheme, and couldn't get anyone to listen. We tried to share the information with the school, for the safety of other students, and again, the individual working security would not listen. Until we can combat non-action and opinions like this, there will not be change.

Chapter 9

Losing It All

You would think with everything I have shared that it would end there. Over time it would get better. Nothing else bad would happen.

Over the course of the next few months I lost almost all of my friends. Today, I have one friend left from that time in my life. One! That is shocking when you think about it. I understand that I would have naturally lost touch with some people. I live in another province now, that makes sense. I don't necessarily blame others for walking away. I changed…a lot. The fearless person I had always been was gone. I had a hard time talking to anyone and I couldn't handle their joy. My life had stopped, but theirs had not.

At the same time, I also expected some people to persevere and push themselves back into my life. After all, that is exactly what I have done for friends who have gone through tough times. But I guess that is not the norm. Acknowledging someone is in pain, letting them have some space, but checking in once in awhile is not what most people do. Either that, or I wasn't worth it. Either way the end result sucked.

My parents convinced me that I needed to tell the individual who had been my best friend for years. Let's call him George. I had been away at school and he was at university in Ontario, a couple hours away from our hometown. We stayed at the "friends" level for longer than we should have, but a long-distance relationship did not make sense me. We had left things a bit in the air at Christmas that year. I was still unsure about distance and what might happen with school. I had transferred universities after my first year and as a result only had five courses left in my last year. Only one or two of those courses were offered in the fall semester, so I looked into options for taking all of my remaining courses from universities closer to home. I was hoping this way I could take most of them in the fall semester. It wasn't looking promising at the time. The school was being difficult about allowing my final courses to be acceptable from other universities, and it wasn't the first time. When I transferred there after my first year, the school would not accept my math credit because it was business calculus and their program required business pre-calculus. I had to take an easier version of calculus for it to count towards my degree. Knowing this, I didn't want to start a relationship where I was half way across the country and we wouldn't see each other for what was looking like almost two years. I could not see how that could work. I had left it that we would wait and talk about it when I was home in the summer and had a better idea of what the year ahead looked like. Everything went back to normal, we still called each other, texted and messaged each other through Facebook. It was constant and I would often get messages from his friends asking when we would just accept that we should be together.

About a year ago some Facebook memories came up from George and his university best friend spamming my Facebook wall with absolute drunken nonsense. I knew them pretty well, so I could always tell who wrote which part of the comments. Sad though that in one phone call everything would change.

Telling George was a mistake…or maybe it wasn't. We had a conversation about what had happened and then I didn't hear from him again until I ran into him a year and a half later. No "How are you doing?" No "I wish I could help." No contact. One of our mutual friends, we will call her Samantha, took his side and told me it was unfair to be out with Tom, a friend they recognized. The assumption was that I was there to make George jealous. That was false. No contact for a year and a half makes it a bit tricky to know where someone is — or to care. I was actually with a group of friends, and was not "with" any of them. I wasn't ready, not that I needed permission from either George or Samantha anyhow. The excuse Samantha gave me for George cutting off contact was "Well, he didn't know how to handle it." Ya, me neither, but I'm glad he had the choice to walk away; I wish I could have, too.

This particular night, I was out with a group that I trusted and as a result was drinking a bit. Get a few drinks in me and I will tell you exactly how I feel about you. I was pissed at the encounter and that George didn't have the balls to talk to me himself. I cornered him and I confronted him. I do not do that often, I actually really dislike confrontation and try to avoid it at all costs. But can I tell you, it felt good. It didn't take long and it simmered down quite quickly. I walked away and continued with my night. Tom had watched me come back. I was shaking, but being an actual friend, he just asked if George and I had finally talked and then we continued on with our night.

George reached out to me the next day and I agreed to talk to him. I let him tell me what happened and how he had freaked out and felt helpless. We talked about how that wasn't the appropriate response, and if he felt helpless, then he should have considered how I might be feeling. He realized he messed up, but he felt it was too late. He mentioned that he had tried to keep tabs on me, but also knew that when I don't want you in my life, I am very good at keeping you out of it. He asked if we could try to be friends again and that he missed having me in his life. I told him I would try, but I didn't think it would be possible. We made plans a couple of times, but it was never the same. I never looked at him the same again. It was too little, too late. I couldn't trust this person because he had already shown me that when I needed him most, he wouldn't be there. That is not a friendship I want.

I wonder sometimes what George told his mom. She always really liked me. She kept our prom picture on hand and would proudly remind us of it every so often, pulling it out to show us. She would always ask what I was up to, and how things were going. She would drink with us before we would go to a party or the bar. I use to stay at his parent's house rather than going home after a night out. I was there a lot. And then all of a sudden, I disappear. Not to be heard from again. What did he tell her? How did he explain that he had just walked away when I needed him most?

In terms of our mutual friend, Samantha, needless to say, while she and I had been close prior to this, we are no longer friends. There really should not have been sides to take. While her and George grew up together, the three of us had been close and would go to the cottage, beach, pool, the bar and parties together. I considered Samantha a close friend. We kept in touch when at school, and the three of us hung out when we were all home. From there it would be whoever else was around, or whomever one of us was dating. It had been that way for awhile.

As a female, I held her to a higher standard. My expectations were that if George had been freaked out and said that to her, that she should have stepped in and been the voice of reason. Instead, she let him spiral. It's not like there was a jealousy factor in there, they were never any more than friends. It wasn't a way to get me out of the picture. For someone who says she is for women sticking up for other women, she doesn't walk the walk.

A few years ago, Samantha started playing ultimate frisbee. It was a couple years after I had started. We saw each other a few times, but the sight of her disgusted me. I would get so angry with her mightier than thou persona and just have to walk away. We obviously do not speak. I wish our ultimate friends didn't overlap.

The part that a lot of people don't know, is that in the months following my assault I didn't leave my house unless a family member was with me. I had panic attacks more often than anyone knew. I had a really hard time sleeping and for the first time in my life, I feared everything. Knowing that, I understand why some people walked away. People need to move on with their lives, and I wasn't living. I was merely surviving and most days that was all I had the strength to do.

I did all of things you are suppose to. I didn't blame myself. I gave my verbal and video statement to police. I completed the rape kit. I was tested. I was poked and prodded at all the right intervals. I went to counselling.

Counselling was important, but not a solution. It was recommended that I go to "talk therapy." I didn't know there were other therapy options. Counselling helped me to talk about a lot of things, many I just couldn't bring myself to discuss with anyone else. The issue was that it required me to live in the past. In the end, while it had its benefits, it didn't "fix me" like everyone thinks it should have. I still have a lot of vulnerabilities and the anniversary each year takes its toll on me. I still retreat and keep the pain I feel during this time to myself. I get very angry sometimes, and I just want to fight. I have almost ruined a couple of friendships that way, so when I feel like that, I distance myself. Other times, I just feel broken. I have already had everyone walk away once, I don't like people to see that side (although they see parts) in case they decide to walk away, too. It doesn't always work, that distance can also push people away.

When I was initially in counselling, I asked specifically for a male counsellor rather than the ones I was offered. My parents supported me. My reason was pretty simple. All the women I came into contact with within the assault unit at the hospital talked to me like I was broken and couldn't be fixed. They always talked with a soft soothing, whisper of a voice. I didn't like that. It made me feel like I was worthless. These were the same women who were in charge of connecting me to the counsellors through their channels. I was put off.

A small portion of my counselling focused on the attack. We talked about it, but I couldn't do anything about it. It couldn't be changed, so the focus for me was on everything else. The first thing I said to my counsellor were my reasons why I had requested a male and that he was not to talk to me like I was broken. We discussed how that wasn't what I needed, and I wouldn't come back if he did.

We talked about how my view on the world changed. We talked about how I was feeling. We talked about how hurt I was that my best friend walked away so easily. I felt abandoned. In the worst time in my life, someone I trusted just left without so much as a goodbye. We also talked about how I felt guilty for all the feelings and issues that were coming up for other family members. Of things in their own past that they had tried to bury. We talked about my panic attacks.

After a while, it just felt like we were constantly talking about the same thing. All I was getting out of the sessions was that my counsellor was impressed that I wasn't blaming myself for the attack. He said that was often the hardest thing for victims. I felt like it was expected that I would be broken and unable to move forward without these sessions. It felt like I wasn't living up to the expectations of a victim. I mean I was, but I was also taking the steps that I needed to not live in this one moment. I recognized the large hurdle and the significant changes that had occurred in my life, but I just wanted to know how to be free of them.

How do you speed up the healing process? You don't.

The time it takes, is the time it takes. I found I was more frustrated that this was out of my control and that expectations were that I would be stuck in this one moment forever.

About half way through our last session, I said, "I think I am done talking." We spent the rest of that session on what I meant by that, and he agreed that I didn't need to come and see him anymore. It was a small thing, but it felt like a step towards rebuilding. It felt like I was released from chains and had permission to start to let go and figure out the new normal.

Counselling didn't stop my nightmares or make me feel less abandoned. It didn't take away the pain or make the physical signs heal any faster. Did it help resolve some issues or provide a safe space to speak? Yes, of course. But the thing is, I no longer needed to talk about it all the time.

One thing we didn't talk about and I wouldn't connect until years later were that a lot of my symptoms were the same as those who suffer from Post Traumatic Stress Disorder (PTSD). Identifying

that in the early years would have helped a lot. My research found
that PTSD symptoms include the following:

- Nightmares
- Guilt/Survivor Guilt
- Poor Judgement
- Intrusive Memories/ Poor Memory
- Flashbacks
- Startle Reflex
- Hypervigilance
- Irritability
- Anger and Rage
- Self Destruction
- Lack of Feelings

- Insomnia
- Poor Concentration
- Hopelessness
- Poor Self-Esteem
- Negative Self-Image
- Apathy
- Mistrust
- Isolation
- Avoidance
- Excessive Blame
- Disassociation

I experienced every symptom on this list in the first year. A number
have dissipated over the years, but I still experience quite a few.
Not all the time, but there are moments when they take over. The
nightmares are the worst. They come and go, but when they come I
never know if there will be just one or if they will continually terrify
me for the immediate future.

The power I felt when I put my symptoms and PTSD together
was unbelievable. It was the first time that I didn't feel alone.
Nine years ago, we didn't talk about the recovery process of
rape and there was no education provided. No one told me I was
high risk for PTSD, and when I connected that I felt stupid. If I
had known there were others feeling the same as me, even if the
reasons behind it were different, I wouldn't have felt like no one
understood me.

My research found this was devastatingly common amongst sexual
assault survivors. The Rape, Abuse & Incest National Network

(RAINN) website says, "94% of women who are raped experience symptoms of post-traumatic stress disorder (PTSD) during the two weeks following the rape."[3] While an American statistic, I still feel it is applicable. Suddenly I felt a bit more normal.

Chapter 10

Panic Attacks

Panic attacks suck. I had never had one before all this happened, but I have had more than I would like to admit since. There were two particularly bad ones.

The first came a few months after my attack. I was working for my stepdad's law firm, testing out if it was something I wanted to do (it was not). It was the end of June, so there were a lot of house closings that day. I was out running between his firm and the law firms on the other side. Being a nice day, a co-worker had given me walking directions to one of the firms. On the way there, one of the local homeless drug addict/drunks who frequented downtown started to follow me. The street I was on had the train tracks on one side and a commercial building on the other, so there wasn't a lot of public view and there wasn't an easy way to re-route. I started to panic.

If you have ever watched the scene in the horror movies where the girl starts to panic and run right before she is killed, that is the image that was going through my mind. Once I was able to get onto a more open street he turned and went the other way. I dropped off the documents at the law firm and made my way back. By the time I was almost back to the office I was drenched in sweat and there was no way I was going back in there to face anyone who didn't know my story. I called the office and had my stepdad meet me up the street. He tried to calm me down. Through tears I asked if I could just go home. I was as pale as could be, and looked like I was about to pass out. He agreed and took me home.

The last one was a couple years ago and was completely avoidable. My friend, Claire, was home for a visit in the summer and wanted to celebrate my birthday, which had been the week before. I had outgrown the bar scene, but she wanted to go out, so that was fine. I think she knew Issacs's best friend was downtown. She had a huge crush on him and was hoping to run into him. Issac and I had dated briefly many years earlier, which is how I became friends with Claire. We ended up running into him, that wasn't an issue, him and I still get along. We don't go out of the way to see each other, but always catch up when we do.

I had recently started seeing Elliot, who Claire had introduced to me at a mutual friend's birthday party four years earlier. I had said no to dating him over the years for various reasons. One being his partying lifestyle and dependence on alcohol. In the recent months he had appeared to have grown out of this, so I agreed to try. It wasn't going well.

As soon as I gave in, he went right back to his old ways. He missed my birthday the previous week because going out drinking the night before was more important. We had made plans for my birthday months earlier, before dating was even on the table. I love waterfalls and, apparently, he did too. We were going to take my dog and go hiking for the day, but he was too hungover. He didn't text or call me, didn't acknowledge my birthday at all.

This wasn't the first time drinking had taken priority. I had watched him time workouts at the gym around when the LCBO closed. There were times he had been fidgety and cut workouts short so he could make it before close. This happened in the middle of a workweek. He didn't think it was a big deal, until I told him that it was exactly why I had said no to him for so long. I told him I didn't want to continue building a relationship if this was how things were going to be.

He was attempting to redeem himself from that, so when he found out I was going out with Claire, he met up with us. When he got there, he went right to the bar and started ordering shots of vodka, four at a time, for himself. I had already switched to water by the time he got there, and was getting ready to go home. He was still drinking and had Claire convince me to stay for a bit longer. We had run into some old friends; fine, I could take one for the team. We stayed until close.

At closing a bunch of this group was going back to Isaac's house to continue drinking. Claire wanted to go, and knowing how drunk she was, I talked to Isaac to make sure he was OK with her going and would make sure she was alright. He is very good about that. Elliot also wanted to go. I did not. I wanted to get home to my dog. She had just been spayed a couple days earlier and was young, so I didn't want to leave her for too long. Elliot said that was fine and he was happy to leave if that is what I wanted.

We said goodbye to the group and started to walk to get a cab. Somehow in all of this, Elliot got himself all worked up that I didn't want to go to Isaac's house. He thought that must mean that there was something going on with Isaac and got ridiculously jealous. He ended up leaving me by myself downtown to take a cab alone. Cabs are triggers for me and Elliot knew this. With a group I am fine, but

alone at night is an entirely different story. Cue flashback to how I was assaulted in the first place, followed by a panic attack.

I was freaking out and having a hard time breathing. I tried to call my brother-in-law to come get me. He had been downtown earlier in the night and had offered to drive me home. We live a street apart. He had left his phone at his buddy's house so didn't get my calls.

I was not the next person in line for a cab, but when next cab arrived, I pulled myself together, walked up to it and talked to the driver. I told him I knew I wasn't next but explained what happened. He understood and could sense the panic in my voice. He told me the group of guys who were approaching could wait and to get in. Luckily, this night ended safely, but it shouldn't have happened. Needless to say, Elliot and I don't speak anymore.

Chapter 11

Starting Over

Something they don't tell you when you are raped, is it isn't just one test that you complete. It is a recurring reminder that someone violated you. I went for my initial rape kit and tests. Not at the ideal time given that I didn't know for almost a day…or didn't accept the reality of it. One week later, another test. At the one-month mark, another. Then at three months, six months and finally a year. I have no qualms about the testing given that it is there for my health. But it was a mentally rough task each time. A reminder each time that a horrific event had happened. The rape centre in my hometown has an undisclosed floor in the hospital. Do you think I ever remembered which floor it was? There was so much anxiety about going that I would blank every time.

By the way, because it is a secured area, you cannot just walk into that wing of the hospital. When you get there, you push the button and wait to be accompanied to the waiting room. I completely understand why it is this way, safety matters. It still turns my stomach to think about the lengths we have to go because of a choice someone else made for us.

My assault occurred April 1 (some April Fools prank, huh?), and it wasn't until January or February of the next year that I would leave my house without a family member. My university coach, who has since passed (he was a great man, I often miss him) had reached out to my local competitive club coach to see how I was doing. No one had heard from me.

My club coach then reached out to a team member, Ann, asking if she had talked to me. Her and I had lost touch after high school, so she thought it was odd and said no. My club coach suggested that she reach out and without telling her what happened, told her I needed someone on my side. So, she did. I didn't take to meeting up right away. My sister is the one who convinced me. She told me to at least try.

If you have ever been on a first date with someone you don't know very well, meeting up with Ann felt a bit like that, but way scarier. It gave me a lot of anxiety and I almost bailed. But I didn't and that was the start to me being able to trust people again. She was smart about it, she started small with people I knew well (her brother and parents) and then slowly added new people to the mix. Slowly, my anxiety of other people and being out of the house started to go away.

No one really knew what I was going through, but they did know it was a bit challenging at first to get to know me. Having already gone through losing all of my friends once, I am slower on the uptake in letting new people in. This can come across as people thinking I am not very friendly, but that is not my intention. I am standoffish in the initial stages and let people come to me to show me who they are. I watch how they interact with others. I listen to how they talk about the friends who are not present. And then I decide if this is someone I want to let in. There are people I cannot trust regardless of how many times we come into contact. I never let my guard down. These individuals tend to only ever see the serious side of me. On the other hand, there are those I am completely comfortable with and get to see all sides. I still have a serious side — I always have — but that is not the only one. I am fun and goofy as well, but unless I feel I can completely trust you; you don't get to see it.

The next big step was going to the gym on my own. That sounds like a simple task, but it wasn't. Initially, I would only go to the gym with my sister. When I was trying to gain back some independence, I started going to the local women's only club by myself. It was a safe space for me by that time. It took months, but eventually I forced myself to go alone to the co-ed gym. It was daunting. Even though I would just be on an elliptical or treadmill and have headphones on, it still took a lot out of me. While I am aware most people are at the gym for themselves and do not take much notice of those around them, I felt like everyone was staring at me, and that I was out of place. I often wanted to just hide in a corner. I didn't, but I wanted to.

I went through different phases during my healing. Initially, all I could do was talk about it, which somehow made it seem less severe. I'm sorry for those who had to listen to me try to rationalize it all away. I tried and I tried hard. Word vomit all over the place. I had it down pat. As long as my family wasn't around, I could talk about it straight faced, without shedding a tear (those would come later). I am not sure why I felt I needed to hide the tears. Trying to show I couldn't be hurt? That I was invincible? That he didn't win? Or maybe I was just trying to make it feel normal. Like something that just happens that you can easily move on from. I couldn't fake it if family was around though. There are still a lot of days now that if a family member is present, I can't get through the discussion without some tears.

I have never been an overly touchy person. Unless you are a select few, I like my distance and my space. This heightened after I was assaulted. I really appreciate the individuals who ask if they can hug me or touch me. That puts me at ease, or at least lets me accept that someone is going to invade my space. I don't promise to like it. It is more likely I will find it awkward, but I can do it. Some days, the answer is still no, others it's OK. For the most part I prefer no contact. It isn't just applicable with friends, acquaintances and strangers, I have the same feelings about family members. One downside is that others take it personally as if it is an attack on them. This is never the intention because my comfort and awareness over what my body does and does not need is just different. I used to try to hide in a corner or sneak out the door, now I just say no. My intentions are not to be cold or seem unloving, but I no longer give in to what others want if it is in conflict with what I need.

This self awareness was hard to learn. I feel bad sometimes when it is my nieces and nephews, but I am sorry I will never be the aunt that kisses you every time I see you. I have no issue if they come up and ask for a hug. I will gladly give it, but then if they get to a point where they do not want the contact either, I am just as OK with a high-five, a wave from a distance or just a hello/goodbye Aunt Tori. It works for me, if it works for them. Now my dog on the other hand, well she is always going to get hugs and kisses from me, but even she asks for them.

Chapter 12

Reconnecting

While I was writing this, Ann and I tried to pin down how we reconnected. We went back through our Facebook history and found the message where she initially reached out. My response to her was one word. From there we do not seem to have another conversation until long after we had started hanging out again.

It is a bit of a mystery, and we think that maybe the messages disappeared. At the time we were messaging back and forth, Facebook messenger did not exist. Messages still went to your "inbox." Neither of us had the other person's phone number either.

It isn't necessarily important how we came back into contact; the important part is we did. I still remember the restaurant and what table we sat at. Ann doesn't remember, but going out in public on my own was a significant event. I lost nine months of freedom because of my assault. Nine months where I didn't feel safe to be alone.

Somewhere along the way I reconnected with some high school friends. I started with just catching up with a couple of them through

Facebook. I was reintroduced to my current best friend, Mary, at a birthday party. We were both high level athletes in our respective sports, so while we had the same group of friends in high school, we were never free at the same time. After that night, we became inseparable. Her parents lived a block away until a couple years ago. Mary and I spent a lot of nights at one another's places.

Mary missed a lot of the bad times, so it is nice to have someone to start fresh with. Because we had not been close in high school I was comfortable being around her, but there was no expectation that I should be a certain way. I was able to continue to heal, while slowly being more open to social events. I stopped freaking out when there was alcohol around. I started to be open to going to parties and the bar again. I started to once again feel comfortable in my own skin.

Mary made it easy to be around her. Unlike some of our other friends, she was just as happy to stay in as to go out. I cannot remember when I told her what had happened, but it wasn't until later in our friendship. It was nice to have someone else in my court that knew the full story and did not judge me for it. She was supportive when I went on my first date after the assault. The first date went OK, but I was not sure how I felt about it. I talked to her about it, and after the second date, which did not go well at all, she was just as supportive and reassured me that I was not overreacting in being upset by the events. Our friendship felt so normal and I had missed normal.

Mary and I often saw each other more than whomever we were dating at the time. We were a bit of a package deal. You couldn't date one of us if the other one didn't like you. While she moved away for graduate school and is now married with kids, we try to stay in touch.

They say when you reach adulthood your friends become fewer, but those who stick around are that much closer to you. I think

I'm Not the Only One

this happened much earlier for me. I have three best friends: Ann, Mary and Alex. It's funny because I have known each of them since middle school, but we became close later in life. One stuck with me through the worst period of my life, one helped me to start living again when I wasn't sure I could, and the third came back into my life when everyone else was running away.

Chapter 13
A New Normal

I became very protective of my family. I knew how much it upset one of my sisters. She had encouraged me to attend the university I went to and when she found out what happened, she also knew which bar. She blamed herself, even though I didn't. She did not make this decision; she did not do anything wrong. For the first month or so, she felt so guilty she couldn't look at me. She felt helpless. It took my mom finding an excuse for her to take me somewhere for her to start to forgive herself. We were in her car, not talking, then all of sudden she turned down the music and said, "I don't know how to make it better. I don't know what to do. You need to tell me what you need."

I never let my family see the bruises, cuts, bite marks, etc. The time of year made it easy to stay covered. Some things took longer than others to heal and I never let on how much pain I was really in, at least physically. I didn't wear my hair up if my sisters were around. They couldn't see the lacerations around my neck.

Each night my immediate family would call. It felt like a phone train. One would call, and as soon as the phone was hung up, someone else would be checking in. Most nights my mom or stepdad handled the calls. Sometimes I would talk, other times I wouldn't.

My dad went right into police mode. He was a cop at one time, he has some involvement now but at a different level. He kept things factual and I think he annoyed the heck out of the police force involved. He worked a lot of sexual assault cases in his day, so when he found out things that weren't done quite right, he was all over it. One of my sisters told me that strings were pulled and he was provided updates on what was going on. I never asked to confirm if that was true.

There came a point in time where I needed everyone to stop. I needed a break, I needed to at least pretend things were normal. They weren't, but fake it until you make it, right?

The next stage was trying to pretend it never happened (read fail). After almost a year, I wanted to be a normal 22-year-old. I tried going out with my friends, which worked for a minute. With some groups it was fine because I knew the plan: go out, crash at someone's house or get a ride home with friends. Never on my own.

I learned to spot the friends who would forget all of your plans and ditch once they got a bit of alcohol in them or met a guy at the bar. I also found that I became protective of them. Over the years, I have made more than one person go back to a bar with me because so and so won't go home, or is having a breakdown or someone had gone home and then showed back up at the bar. If I wasn't completely sober, I would find a ride (always with someone) and if I was sober, I would drive to get them. That is just the way it was.

Going out wasn't as fun. If I don't know enough people around me, I am very uptight and nervous the entire time. I have been the DD on numerous occasions, just because that is an easy excuse.

During this time, I also tried to convince myself (as did those around me) that I was ready to date. I was not. I failed many times. I went on a "date" with a friend that I didn't know was a date. When I clued in, I said goodbye and quickly put as much distance between us as possible. I literally ran to my car and left as quickly as possible. Yes, that happened. Sorry! We never talked about it. We just moved on like it never happened. We are still friends but let's just say there was never an attempt at a do-over.

I had become friends with David, one of the guys in our group. I was straight up with him that I couldn't handle anything more than being friends. He didn't want to hear it and didn't understand. He thought it was a game. Nope, this was my life. He wouldn't listen to explanations and would wave it off, changing the subject any time I tried to explain. He didn't want to hear that assaults were real, he couldn't handle the reality of it. He eventually blamed me, saying I was a tease. David distanced himself and left me alone for awhile.

When he thought I was ready to start dating he persisted to drunk text me and tell me how much he liked me, trying to get me to come out in the middle of the night. My response was always the same: "Ask me on a real date" or "Tell me how you feel when you are sober, I'm not a backup plan." However, when anyone else was around, David would try to pawn it off as being me and avoid me. Maybe not the nicest guy. My main friend group at this time included him, so I learned to not let him get to me. He later set me up with one of his friends, and then got mad because I went on a couple of dates with him.

Then there were the times where things started to progress but I wasn't ready. The first time I attempted to let someone get close to me, and intimate, I ended up in another panic attack. It isn't fun to end up in the fetal position, rocking back and forth hoping to calm down fast. It's extremely embarrassing and there is no right way out of it. It's just bad. Everyone feels awful, feelings are hurt, moments are awkward, and figuring out how to end that situation is excruciating.

Eventually, I stopped dating or even trying, which didn't help either. Random people would be perplexed and wonder why I was single, trying to identify my major flaw. I was told "Someone is out there for you" over and over again. I wish I could have yelled, "I want to throw up every time someone mentions sex or tries to touch me!" but that doesn't pair well with dating and relationships.

The idea that being single makes you flawed or weak is a bit disgusting and this conversation needs to change. Our worth should not be decided based on our relationship status. I know a lot of people in toxic relationships. I have never needed the reassurance that "Someone is out there for me" because it always makes me feel bad about myself. The thing is, happiness should not come from another person. I like myself the way I am. There have been others in and out of my life, but if they take away from how I feel about myself, why should I stay or want that? To make you feel better?

Often times those who have said that to me, do not know anything more about me than that. They know I am a very motivated and determined individual, but they do not know what I have seen or experienced. I have been told that I should lower my standards because I am starting to get too old to have children. I am not a baby making factory, that is not the only thing that I am good for. Maybe that isn't in the cards for me, but that is OK. To tell me that I need to settle is not respectful and is also not healthy.

I am a bit harder to be in a relationship with because of what I've been through. I have seen the fear and watched those who are not strong enough to handle my past run away. I have mostly good days, but the bad days are tough. I can tell when the bad days are coming, but I also get hit with surprises. Mostly these are due to unexpected triggers. I can only do so much to stop anything from triggering me. There have been years where I had none, but then something happens and they come back. That is beyond my control, but unless the other person is strong enough and able to hold on throughout those times, it is actually worse for me when they walk away during it.

Mental health issues are also a new normal. In the initial days, everyone who knew what was going on kept tabs on me. They constantly checked-in and offered or asked how they could help me out. As time went on, being aware of my metal wellbeing and asking for help when needed became more on me. I do not have an issue with that. As I became stronger, I could take back the responsibilities of being an adult. This is one that many of us struggle with. It is a bit of a catch 22: you want people to treat you normally, but in doing so, you need to step up, take ownership and do something about it when you are having a hard time. Knowing when you need more help than you can provide to yourself is a challenge in itself.

In the first few years after I was raped, I felt guilty each year when the anniversary came around. It was the reminder that I gave up. That is how I would remember it. I would feel guilt for not being stronger and going through with the court case. For being selfish in wanting to move forward with my life. That took its toll on me that time of year. I would get very irritable and be difficult to be around. I would snap quite easily and isolate myself whenever I could.

After about year three, I had a little bit of anxiety in February, but it would only last a couple of weeks and was not much of anything. Then #metoo happened. Everything I had buried came rushing back. It was hard to avoid it. Sexual assaults and rapes were getting more attention, media was following the stories and reporting on them. It was becoming less taboo. All of these are good things.

However, when you are used to pushing away the feelings because no one wants to hear about it, you get accustomed to one way of living. Overnight it changed. We started to wake up a little bit, and it seemed like maybe finally society was ready to change. The movement gained some traction, some people became more aware. The process had started, some of us were ready. Like all forms of change we still have an uphill battle ahead of us. For me that battle includes revisiting times I would like to forget. Talking about what happened to stir those who just need that extra push to understand means allowing myself to feel the pain all over again. I will do it, but in doing so I need to be smart and take care of my mental health, too.

When you have a cold or the flu, those around you understand. They can see it and process that you are not feeling great. I have anxiety and a lot of it. To be more correct, as I mentioned, I have actually been diagnosed with PTSD just like many other survivors. I am not unique in this regard, but we all handle our symptoms differently. I alluded to this earlier, but the worst symptom is the nightmares. Sometimes it is just one. Other times it is every night for an extended period of time. When these longer periods happen, I end up in a state where I cannot sleep at all. The nightmares are not always a direct re-playing of the assault, but I am severely injured or killed in each one. Just so you know, you can watch yourself die in your sleep and still wake up. As an adult, explaining that you get nightmares is not something people take seriously, but it is very common with PTSD. The issue isn't the theme of the nightmares, it is the feelings and emotions they cause.

One nightmare is manageable, but when they are on repeat, it is very difficult to not have them interfere with the rest of my life. They heighten my anxiety and bring out some OCD symptoms. At the worst of it, my doctors prescribed a low-dose of an anti-anxiety/anti-depressant to help.

I likely should have started on medication years sooner, but like a lot of people mental health is not something I am overly comfortable discussing. It was embarrassing to ask for help. I had been debating for a long time because I perceived taking medication as being weak. I am very stubborn, and independent. I worked so hard to get my independence back, and I struggled with the thought that if I needed assistance it meant I was not strong enough. It was like everything I had done meant nothing.

One day I was adding up the different ways my PTSD and anxiety were holding me back. When it comes to relationships, that is when it can be the worst and the most noticeable. Every bad situation that could possibly occur plays out in my head. Every way I could be viewed as a terrible person. Every way I could be hurt. I often have myself convinced that when someone does show interest, that it is just a big joke. That somewhere he is tracking all the ways he can convince me that this is real, and then pull the rug out from under me. It is not a great situation to find yourself in.

Other ways that my anxiety has started to come out was with locking my car doors. I have to hit the lock button on my car twice. If the car does not beep, I will not stop wondering if my car is locked. If my car did not beep at me after the second time, who knows how many times I would lock it.

If I am the first car before the crosswalk at a stoplight, I watch the individuals crossing the road. If there is no one in the car with me, and someone looks at me, I lock my car doors. Do you really think the pedestrian cares about me? Unlikely. I am not that important. For the most part I drive during the day. Who is going to try to get into my car when there are witnesses everywhere?

Part of the problem is that I know how unreasonable my reactions are, but I cannot stop them. I have never been someone who sits and worries about things. I never liked to get in trouble when I was younger, but I was also tempted by so many things that I would often do things and ask for forgiveness later. You knew when I did not like something. My family still tells the story of me "running away." Here's the catch: I was mad because I was not getting my way, so I packed up my yellow briefcase with my blankie, my teddy bear and some crayons, put it on the back of my tricycle and rode away. I meant business. My family stood at the bottom of the driveway and waved me off, but I was determined to win this battle. I was going to go to the ends of the Earth. They would miss me. Then I ran into a problem…I was only allowed to go as far as the base of the hill, which was about the distance of 4-5 driveways. So that ruined my whole plan. I wanted to be mad, and for them to pay, but I also knew the rules. I am sure I thought about going farther but getting in trouble did not seem worth it. And now here I was years later, coming up with new ways that life was out to get me. I was frozen and unable to get past the endless possibilities of unfortunate events, however unlikely.

One day I decided I would just take a drive and if the walk-in clinic did not have too long of a wait I would see what the doctor had to say. I was giving myself an out. I did not have an appointment I needed to keep, I could change my mind and not walk through the door. The line was not long, but I felt out of place in the waiting room. Everyone else had a cold and here I was, looking pretty terrible, but healthy, and making them wait a bit longer.

The doctor walked in and I started to cry. It turns out I am a bigger crier than I would like to admit. Anytime I have to talk about my mental state with a doctor, I cry. It just happens and I wish it did not. It took him all of one minute to diagnose that it was not anxiety alone and walk through my options.

The last time, I was on the medication for four months and it successfully stopped the symptoms but had a lot of negative side effects. I would get headaches really easily. When I first started taking it I would get one everyday within the first 20 minutes. At first, I also lost interest in food, but then as my body became used to the medication, I gained 15 lbs. Considering I was more active and had not changed my diet, it is safe to say this was from the medication. The medication would also make me drowsy, which wore off but I would still be very tired at night and need to go to bed early. While the nightmares stopped, I was restless and not getting a full night's sleep.

I went back to see the doctor and he suggested adding a sleeping pill. I was told to be careful because they are highly addictive, but I thought to myself there is no way I am going down this route. I tried melatonin for awhile, and went with the higher dose, but that wasn't helping. I stopped taking the medication and after a week or so started sleeping better again.

I have only recently admitted to family that I have anxiety. I think the first time I said it out loud was last year. I have never gone into any more detail than that. It is one thing to say anxiety, that is vulnerable enough. To say it is actually PTSD? No thanks. I do not think they all believe me. That is OK though because it also means I do not get asked too many questions. A lot of questions lead to having to explain myself.

Chapter 14

Taking Back Control

Eventually my mind and body were ready to get back to life as a twenty-something. It was a relief but I really did not want to go through another embarrassing situation. This time it was about control and not emotions. I dated a few different people, but I never really invested in them. It was always just about knowing that I had control over my body and that someone couldn't hurt me like that ever again. It was never about a connection with these individuals or letting them get close to me — that wasn't the point. If they did get attached, I cut them off right away. None of the individuals I dated during this period were people I would bring home to my family. Most of them were not overly nice people and I knew they weren't going to last. When you feel somewhat worthless, you attract those qualities. I have done that over and over again. I would eventually come to my senses and look for higher quality individuals, but it took me a long time to get there. It's not my favourite phase, but it is important to understand the full process I went through to move forward.

One real winner was around off and on for three years. I should have walked away day one, but I really believed that he was better than being alone. He wasn't. It started out OK, but he is a master manipulator and he knew just what to say to me to keep me around. He may be the only person I have ever known who can manipulate me so easily. However, I honestly don't understand why you would want to be with someone you have to trick into staying.

At one point he told me that what happened to me wasn't something to be upset about. He told me that his high school depression was much worse. That I should just get over it. I am going to go out on a limb here and say those aren't exactly things you can compare. It should never have been a competition over who had it worse in the first place, and yes, that is a definitely a red flag that should have sent me running. I walked away a few times, but until about a year ago it didn't stick. He tried to come back into my life once again and I agreed to hear him out, but it was the wake up call I needed. This time, as he was trying to tell me how much he missed having me in his life and about how terrible his most recent ex was, I just looked at him and knew I deserved better.

Maybe I have never had the healthiest of relationships. I remember being in love with a boy when I was a teenager but our relationship was toxic and we fought most of the time. We were both athletes of the same sport and trained together every day. While we went to different schools, that was about the only time we had a break from each other. During the years of that relationship, I cried myself to sleep a lot of nights. Everything was somehow always my fault, and I hated that, but I was afraid of losing him. I was so invested in the idea of him, that I would have done anything to make it work. He was almost two years older than me and our relationship matured faster than I did. I always felt pressure to match his expectations. That's how it starts: one partner not being satisfied with where things are. Needing more, expecting more, chipping away at you little by little.

I'm Not the Only One

In the beginning it wasn't like this. In the beginning we respected each other. Then, we slowly took each other for granted. We fought more and got a bit nastier each time. Eventually we couldn't take the words back.

It was the worst around Christmas time. His mom had passed away from cancer when we were quite young. He had been close with her and never really accepted her death. Her passing was right before Christmas and he would get angry at the world and at me. The pain of her memory would be taken out on everyone he came into contact with, with me getting the brunt of it. I let him, knowing what was really causing it, but as a teenager I still took it personally.

About a year into our relationship I had a significant back injury. It took the year for different medical professionals to finally determine what was causing the pain and start the process of rehabilitation. I had been one of the top athletes in the country for my age group, and one of the youngest athletes competing at the national level meets. I was on track to make the junior teams, but my injury changed all of that. My back broke into spasms any time hard training or speed was required. Some days I trained for an hour, some for 20 minutes and other days I was in too much pain before even getting out of bed. I was sent home from school often. Any classroom that had stools rather than chairs was 90 minutes of torture.

During this time, he was breaking through in his events. I had made junior nationals the year before him, and while I was not competing very well this year, I still qualified. Even though he knew how injured I was, and how hard of a time I was having with not being able to compete, he would still rub it in my face that he had six junior national standards and I only had three. Up until this point I had also been better than him at my best events, so he also made it his mission that year to top me in those. It was going to happen at

some point — nature of male anatomy versus female anatomy — but the timing was brutal.

As this went on, he also started forcing himself on me. He was bigger and stronger, so I really didn't have a chance. I was so confused on how I was supposed to feel about the situation. On the one hand I was in love with him and wanted him around all the time. On the other hand, I was conflicted and torn. I felt like there was something wrong with me. As much as I loved him, I didn't want to be pinned under him. I felt forced to "be ready" when I was not. I felt like it was my only choice. That is a hard thing to grasp and understand and I am not sure I do today. I never considered what he did to be rape because most of the time he would have me pinned with clothes still on. I did eventually give in to his pleas before I was ready, but that was a choice I made, so that always had me at odds with myself. I eventually coped by finding ways to hurt myself. I would pull my nails off a little too much, to the point where the skin would bleed slightly and it would be sensitive for a few days. I would take a mini pocket knife to my skin. Not to cut and bleed out, just to poke my skin a bit so that I was in control of the pain.

We eventually broke up…at a national competition, on my birthday.

I bring up that story because I have had a couple of conversations recently about how early experiences in life shape us. My first relationship was emotionally trying and physically abusive. I did not accept it at the time, but that is what it was. I am not convinced that was the intention on his part. I do not think he set-out for it to be that way, but maybe that is just me being naïve. I like to think that being teenagers who went through some tough times had a lot to do with it. That did, however, impact what I thought relationships were for a very long time. Maybe some days I still do. I would have a hard time accepting that guys could be nice to me. I always assumed the worst and, in a way, sought it out.

Chapter 15

Moving Forward

There is one important aspect to my story that only a couple of people know: I found out who did this to me. That is a difficult statement to put in writing. I felt like if I just knew in my mind, that maybe it wasn't real. The worst part was, he recognized me, too.

As I mentioned earlier, I was asked to decide whether I would press charges while I was still in shock. I had no idea, so the police officer did nothing. This resulted in losing all of the evidence that could have been available from my room. My dad says it should have been gathered anyway. I've heard the same from another individual with a policing background. I'm not police, I don't pretend to know. To me though, that logically makes sense. I would think in any other situation, evidence is collected before the police even know if charges are being laid.

Once the shock of what had happened wore off, I considered pressing charges. I questioned what this would look like given this crucial evidence was missing. One of the things I struggled with was "What if they find the wrong guy?" I wanted the individual responsible to pay for what he did — I wanted him to feel the pain. I don't hate many people, but I do hate him. I don't consider myself a violent person, but the thoughts of ways he could suffer have gone through my mind. Our judicial system is not enough. It seems like the easy way out. The thing is, as much as I wanted that, I also feared the wrong person might take the blame. My mind has blanked him out. I know his voice, but other than the security tape, which is not the best quality, I don't remember anything about his features. This fear of someone else taking the blame haunted me.

I did my research on sexual assault court cases and as much as they say they don't attack the victim, to me it seems like they do. I had already been attacked enough. I didn't think I could go through my character also being questioned. Being told that it was somehow my fault would have broken me.

A stronger pull against trial was the security video. I had to watch it and I never wanted anyone in my family to see it. I held strong through the video — meaning I cried a lot. I tried to give my statement of it through a mess of emotions. When I left, I was shaking, it was hard to breathe and I vomited.

I couldn't get past being in court, having my character put on trial and on top of that making my family watch the video. I already knew there were several things that were going to work against me. After the assault, I had showered. I didn't get a drug test done soon enough to show strong evidence, not enough evidence was taken by the officer, the scene was disrupted, the cab companies all denied any rides to my address.

My family could tell I was swaying and having a hard time deciding what to do. I really wanted to move on with my life, but at the same time was grappling with the idea that I had to go through with the court case. I already knew the result: a he said, she said argument.

I'm Not the Only One

Without the additional evidence I was going to lose and have my character ripped apart in the process. On top of that, my family would have to see the video. The legal process was going to cause even more pain to me and my family, so while an unpopular choice, I chose to let it go.

Once I did that, I felt free. Not in the sense that I could just go back to "normal" but in that I could breathe. It was the first time that I allowed myself to look forward to what my life could be, rather than back at what I couldn't change. I was still healing, still keeping panic attacks a secret and still struggling to let people in. I was trying, but it was hard.

I chose not to go back to my university for my final year. Instead, I made arrangements with my university to take my remaining courses from schools close to home. They were approved prior to enrollment so that I knew they would count towards my degree and I would be able to graduate. I had been double majoring, but due to one course not being available online or at any other university, I had to drop one of my majors. It still bugs me a little bit that I am just one course short, but it happens. In the grand scheme of things, it doesn't really matter anyway. I was focusing on a major in supply chain and logistics and another in marketing management, yet today I'm an accountant. Vastly different.

Because I was at home for my last year of school, I did not get the chance to have my grad photos taken during the year. Instead, when it came time for graduation, we added a couple extra days to the trip so that I could do them then. There were a couple of photographers in the city that had the business school robes, and I chose one of them. I was dropped off at my scheduled time, and my family left to tour the city. Once I was there, everything seemed normal. I waited in the reception until it was my turn. Once they were ready for me, the assistant took me in and set me up. The photographer came in shortly after, said a couple of things and I immediately knew.

A panic attack started. The graduation photos were important to my family, so I tried to keep it together. He took some photos. By this time, I was sweating profusely, hoping it wasn't noticeable, but knowing it likely was. I could feel my hair starting to stick to my face, but I was frozen. I couldn't think. All I could do was turn my head the way he suggested. It wasn't until the end that he made a comment about knowing who I was. He did not come right out and say it, but it was implied.

I was embarrassed by the whole thing. I had no idea what I was walking into. It was a hot summer day, so when my family picked me up, I let on that I was hot from the building not having air conditioning and being outside for awhile. I am either freezing cold or boiling hot so no one questioned me any further and I was OK with that. I have never told my family that is why I do not have graduation photos. For awhile they asked if they could see the prints, but I just told them that because of the lack of AC my prints were awful and there was no way Photoshop would be able to fix them. They eventually stopped asking.

I have been asked why I did not go to the police and report him right then and there. To be honest, it didn't even cross my mind as an option. When you go through a panic attack you are not thinking clearly. Your mind goes blank, and all you see is your fear. And I mean *see* it. It is hard to explain but if you have experienced a panic attack you may find it easier to understand why I didn't call the police.

In all of the time after, I never had the thought. I think because of how evidence collection had gone early on, it was not on my mind that I could revisit it. By the time of the photo shoot, the only physical evidence had been destroyed. I had already had the call to tell me that six months was up, so my rape kit was gone. To then go back and say I found him — this is the man who raped me — it just seemed so improbable that it was never much of a consideration. Again, it would have been another scenario of he said, she said. And when it comes to sexual assault, she doesn't win.

I was also asked why I did not inform the university. Again, in the frame of mind I was in, the goal was to get distance and make sure I was safe. You can judge me for that, call me stupid or lazy or selfish, but it wasn't something I thought of. A rational person has the advantage of thinking logically and making sense of right and wrong, good and evil. When it comes to my experience I just can't. It was not even until I started the process of writing this book and was talking to arm's length individuals who questioned me on that, that it even dawned on me that I could have done something.

Since then I have looked up the street his studio was on to see if it was still there and I could find the name. It isn't there anymore. I have looked on the university's website to see if they listed the photographers that they use and see if any name triggers anything for me. None of the names seemed familiar. I did try, but I waited too long. I feel like I am supposed to apologize for not thinking of other options. That I let people down in this regard. It was not a conscious decision, and one that seems so obvious now that it has been pointed out. That is a guilt that has been placed on me by individuals who did not experience my assault and possessed a clear thought process. I made my decision based on the information I had in front of me. Not everyone will understand that.

Chapter 16

Family Impact

I have talked about my experience as the survivor of the assault, but I was not the only victim. My family was impacted, too. They had to figure out what to do and say, and also how to continue on with their lives while trying to help me.

My parents have been divorced since I was in Grade 1. They had shared custody of my sisters and I, but we predominantly lived with our mom. After I made the call to my mom, she did the rest. She called my dad first to tell him what happened. It was late at night and they generally do not speak except for at special functions, so he already knew it wasn't good that she was calling.

I didn't talk to my dad until I was home. I didn't talk to anyone else in my family, actually. The way he handled it was going into police mode. I know he wanted me to press charges, and if I thought it would have made a difference I would have. I do not think I ever outwardly told him that I chose to drop them, but I know he knows.

My sisters, Michelle and Lynn, found out in a two-minute phone call. My mom got off the phone with me and called them. From what I have been told the conversation went something along the lines of: "We're going to get Tori, she's been raped. You need to take care of the animals until we get back." Click.

The biggest frustration for Michelle and Lynn was that they couldn't do anything and didn't know how to help. I have talked to both of them about things they wish they had known or could have asked and both get stuck on knowing what to do. They both felt so helpless.

They both said they felt defeated by not having the right answers or questions to ask. They didn't know what the right or wrong thing to do was. The thing is, there is no guidebook. Lynn (who is a teacher) has mentioned multiple times that she finds it frustrating that our society wants to avoid the topic of sexual assault. She has been asked not to talk about it more than once.

Michelle and Lynn spent some time together afterward to help each other and figure out if there was anything they could do. They brainstormed and came up with the original idea for a side project we have. I cannot go into any more detail because it includes proprietary information, but they brought me in right away, since well…it is because of me.

Lynn and I talked about her fears. She is raising two boys and also billets hockey players for the semi-pro hockey team in town. She fears one of the players will be wrongly accused as the last individual a girl in the bar remembers if she is drugged. I understand this fear because it is similar to the one I had about the wrong person being convicted of assaulting me. It is a valid fear. I tried to explain that this is the reason why we need to remove the stigma around sexual

assault. Not only does it protect women, but it also protects men….
if done correctly.

If the stigma goes away, then the fear around being believed is
removed. This increases the chances of a rape kit. If the DNA is
not there, then the player can be remembered, but the evidence
will not match. There should also be security cameras at bars to
narrow down the search. Preventative measures require opening
the conversation on a wider scale. We can more effectively educate
people about what consent is — when it is OK to move forward,
and when you should wait. Until we educate everyone on the issue,
we will face challenges. Obviously, this is an over simplification,
but you can see the thought pattern. It comes down to awareness,
education and safety measures.

Lynn and I also have differing opinions on how to approach it with
teenage girls in schools. I understand why she wants to educate
girls on how the way they dress is important. I get that, but I
also disagree…in the delivery. Right now, the school boards and
administration are focused on dress codes in our schools. The thing
is, when I relate back to my own experience, it was never that I had
an issue with having a dress code, it was that I had an issue with it
not being evenly distributed.

Just like in a workplace, there is appropriate attire for school. Bums
do not need to be hanging out, for example. My issue was never
so much with the attire, but that only girls were called out. When
I was in high school, one of the trends with the boys was "wife
beater" shirts and jeans that stopped under their bum. First, let's
just acknowledge the issue with openly calling this shirt a "wife
beater." That has its own set of negative connotations. It wasn't
a great look but that was the style. I went to a school with no air
conditioning. In June it gets stuffy and hot. As a teenage girl with
hormones changing all the time, temperature regulation was an

issue. OK — I was sweaty and it was embarrassing. As someone who has always dressed more conservatively, I tried to follow the dress code and usually succeeded. While I was never called out for being against the dress code, I wasn't impressed when teachers called out girls for wearing tank tops that were not wide enough, and shorts that were too short and showed their bum. Yet, the boys who wore similar wife beaters and wore their pants low were fine. It didn't make sense. If we are going to have a dress code, apply it equally. We hear this over and over again, but when are school administrators going to understand that the big issue is the application not the intent.

Lynn would like to help girls protect themselves by educating them on the way they dress. For so long, we have had a one-sided discussion on dress, and on defenses against rape that, until we break it all down, rebuild and change our delivery, students are not going to listen. I wouldn't. On the other hand, what you wear does not provide consent, so I have an issue with using the discussion as a means of protection. A means of self-value? Yes, I am for that. The intent behind the delivery matters.

During the initial days, my family and I also talked about who we would and would not tell. In terms of family it was mostly on my terms. I did not want more than our immediate family involved and calling. I asked that it be left to me to decide if and when they needed to know. We discussed how we were not going to tell my grandparents. This was a request of both my mom and dad. All of my grandparents have had health battles, and at the age they are at, we did not want to give them something they could not do anything about but would fixate on and spend days thinking about. I just wanted a normal granddaughter relationship with them while I had that opportunity.

My mom and stepdad let his parents know. They weren't going to, but his parents were moving across the country, and would be moving in with us until their new house was built. At the time, this was still all very new and there were calls coming in from the police, as well as constant check-ups on me from family. I also had quite a few appointments and was not in the best state of mind. In that situation it was the right thing to do.

My sister, Michelle, walked away from a friendship because of how her values and beliefs were impacted by my assault. A couple years after I moved home and was trying to heal, her friend was dating a man who had been found guilty of sexual assault. It is interesting that he still says he was "accused of something he didn't do." No, you were found guilty. Also, it came to light that a couple years later he was an executor of his father's estate and stole the money meant for his brother. He lost his license with his professional board and is no longer allowed to practice, soooo...I am going to go with not a great individual or a reliable source.

Anyway, he was granted leniency by the courts and given a conditional discharge. To Michelle's friend, this meant he was innocent. That is not what it means at all. The *Steps to Justice* website says:

If you get a conditional discharge:

- *you will be on probation for up to 3 years.*
- *your record of discharge will be kept on file for 3 years.*

Your record of discharge is automatically removed after 1 or 3 years, depending on the type of discharge. You do not have to ask to have the record removed.

A *discharge that is still on file can impact your life in many ways. For example:*

- You may not be able to get jobs working with vulnerable people, such as children or the elderly.
- You may not be able to get jobs that require security clearance.
- You may not be able to travel or have problems when you do.
- The police may treat you differently if they know you have a record of discharge.
- Some countries may not recognize conditional discharges as non-convictions. You may be treated as though you have a conviction when traveling to these countries.

If you're convicted of a new crime during your probation, your discharge can be revoked. Instead of the discharge you had before, you can be given a conviction that results in a criminal record, and a new sentence.[4]

Instead she chose to stand by this man and support him, even though she knew her best friend's sister had recently been raped and the trauma that it brought to not only my life, but also Michelle's. What made matters worse, was her friend was in management at a well-known children's organization at the time. She knew the risks associated with this relationship and chose to put everything on the line. For the sake of the children, I hope he was kept away from them.

I do not understand how we convince ourselves of such nonsense. This is another real-world example of just how much we do not understand about sexual assault and rape. It's another instance where the guilty are given special treatment and their violence is excused by those around them.

I heard stories of individuals in our circle who were molested by a family member as children. In one instance, this individual's mother never believed her, and instead turned against her. The issue is that they do not want to accept that this can happen within their own family. I hear about family turning on those children and blaming them. They are left feeling powerless, but I can see how it would be difficult to cut ties and walk away. For this individual, the news of my rape brought up memories and issues for her. It brought back all of the pain of childhood, as well as the negative impact it had on the family dynamic. How do you forgive that?

My brother-in-law doesn't like to talk about what happened. I understand that, none of us do. He did talk to me about a university friend of his. She had been molested by an uncle as a child and had a lot of difficulty around men after that. They had been good friends, and he remembers how hard it could be when they went to the bar. She would go if he did, but if he left to use a washroom, go to the bar, or talk to a friend without her knowing where he was, she would have a panic attack. She was very uncomfortable and untrusting around men. I can completely understand what that feeling is like. It is one reason why bars became less fun for me afterwards. It is so hard for others to understand. You hear things like "not everyone is like that." The thing is, when you have been through trauma, rationalization doesn't help. When you have already encountered evil, you never forget it.

It also brought up issues with one of Lynn's ex-boyfriends. He is an individual we do not like to talk about. Lynn actually won't. He tormented Michelle while he was dating Lynn. On one occasion, he told Michelle he was going to strip her naked and lock her outside for the boys to see. He said this in front of Lynn. Michelle and I have had this conversation and she stated how what hurt the most was that Lynn did not do or say anything. She just sat there. Michelle points out that it took her a long time to get over, but now that she is older, she reflects on it and can't imagine how bad things must have been for Lynn. It must have been pretty bad if you cannot stand up for the ones you love. After that, Michelle use to lock herself in a room if he was in the house and my parents were not home. My parents obviously did not know about this and I did not find out until after my assault. I was too young at the time.

I had quite a few informal conversations with Michelle. We see each other the most, and we would just start talking about the book. In the early stages, Michelle was adamant that she wanted to write something for my book, but she told me as much as she wanted to, she just couldn't get the words on the page. It was after my book had gone in for its initial set of edits that she shared how she had a very similar story to me, but that it turned out differently for her.

Our hometown holds a music festival each year and Michelle and her friends went one year. She was drinking and remembers that while she drank the same amount as her other female friends, she seemed to be more impacted. She recounts losing control of her body and not understanding what was happening. She remembers that it didn't feel right, and she had never reacted to alcohol like this before or since. She remembers how sick she was and that her friends took her home. Like me, Michelle wasn't one to have day-long hangovers, yet this time she was so violently ill the next day. She told me how it took hearing my story and my description of how I felt to accept that she had been drugged.

In this case, her friends noticed right away that something was wrong and got her out of there safely. She is grateful for having the right people around her and recognizing that they needed to get her home. Her story could have easily been the same as mine.

I had conversations with both of my sisters about current TV shows. They both have children and have pointed out some perceptions they have made watching children's shows. One that was mentioned was *Splash N' Boots*. Both of them hate this show, but have watched

I'm Not the Only One

it with the kids. There is a song called *Shake It* on the show where the female character dresses up like a granny and sings a song that teaches little kids how to shake their bum. The lines of the song are:

> *Good Morning Granny. Shaking your bum is what you do.*
> *Good Morning Granny. Let's dance along with you.*
> *I'm the lady with the moves. Come on Granny, show us your grooves.*
> *Shake it. Shake your bum. You gotta shake your bum.*
> *Shake it. Shake your bum. You gotta shake your bum.*

Each time this song is featured on the show, which seems to be a lot, the screen zooms in to focus on her bum. This is a show for two-year olds. Why are they being taught this? I understand that this is not sexual, but this is a very susceptible age group and they copy everything. My niece loves being the centre of attention (what two-year-old doesn't?) and her go to dance moves are always based off of what she watches on TV. She now dances by turning to her audience and shaking her bum.

Of course, she is adorable and just looking for a laugh, but my sister and her husband do their best to not display that with her and ask the rest of the family to do the same. The reasoning is pretty simple: while it is funny today, it won't be when she is 15. My sister does not want to raise her daughter to seek attention in what could later be construed as negative attention. She questions at which stage this goes from cute to sexual. Yes, that is not today, but it is a principal of not wanting to accept a behaviour today and then tell her tomorrow it is no longer appropriate. Today it is a laugh from anyone willing to watch, but it is now engrained that shaking your bum is a way to get the attention you are looking for. If tomorrow that attention is from the boy, my sister wants to raise her daughter that she looks for attention in more positive manners and not rely on her body to do it for her. In addition, since so much responsibility is on girls' actions and not on boys' responsibilities, my sister also wants to teach this so that it reduces the chances of her daughter ending up in a situation where someone says she was "asking for it" and takes things too far. I know how ridiculous that sounds, but that is the point. My family feels that because the responsibilities of others are so weak when it comes to sexual assault and rape, that we are collectively trying to think of anything that will help our family members maintain control and be safe.

Michelle is an avid basketball fan, but she has also become pretty disgusted with how we treat athletes like gods. A player that she has particular issue with is Kobe Bryant. He was a great basketball player, but he is still being celebrated even though he is a convicted rapist. He is a Hollywood A-lister. Nike still sponsored him. Fans still adore him. Everyone is choosing to forget what he did. They shrug their shoulders and say that is ancient history. He isn't the exception; this is the norm. While not an exhaustive list, a few other athlete rapists come to mind: Greg Hardy, Ben Roethlisberger and who could forget Mike Tyson?

The consensus of what I heard was that they wanted the stigma around sexual assaults to go away. I agree. We need to talk about it and hear the stories. We need to realize that this isn't something that is made up or said to gain attention. While I am sure there is a small percentage that do, you can say that about everything.

Chapter 17

Self-Care

One thing I have learned during all of this is how important self-care is. Being able to identify what we need is important in every aspect of our lives. We can use this for everyday things, not just for trauma.

Over the years I have used different forms of self-care. What works for me today is not necessarily what worked for me yesterday. I adapt my strategies and remind myself that sometimes the hardest part is taking the first step.

There are many different forms of self-care, and what works for me may not work for another survivor. They come in the different types: physical, emotional, social, spiritual, personal, space, financial and work. Some examples are:

Physical
- Getting enough sleep
- Being physically active (walking, recreational sport, yoga, etc)
- Choosing healthy food options

Emotional
- Managing stress levels
- Allowing yourself to forgive
- Showing compassion and kindness

Social
- Knowing your boundaries
- Having the support system you need
- Communication

Spiritual
- Allowing yourself to have time alone
- Having a safe space
- Meditation, yoga & connection

Personal
- Having hobbies
- Knowing yourself
- Allowing yourself to be your true self

Space
- Feeling safe
- Living in a healthy environment
- Having security and stability

Financial
- Budgeting and money management
- Paying bills on time
- Saving and having goals

Work
- Time management
- Setting work boundaries
- Having a positive work environment

Some of these are easier than others, and I know for myself that when one of these is off-balance, other areas tend to follow.

For example, when work is stressful, I am tired when I get home and would prefer to just have an easy meal. Easy meals are usually not healthy for me. Not that there aren't healthy options, but easy at this point is anything that does not take effort.

There are times where I have to force myself to pick one thing. Work boundaries are the hardest ones for me because work seems to creep in everywhere. Allowing myself to turn off my email in the evening and on the weekends is difficult.

Checking in on yourself and what you need is a crucial step. Forgiveness is something I am still working on. I will admit, I do not believe that I will ever forgive my attacker. Part of that is because I don't believe he deserves it.

That being said, I allow myself to move forward. Acceptance of the past was difficult. Most of the time I do not dwell on it. Most of the time I continue to live. There are triggers though, and they can pull me right back. I no longer live in the darkness of what happened to me, but that is not to say that there are never reminders.

I have mentioned that counselling was important. Unfortunately, it requires you to continually live in the past, particularly talk therapy. That may help some to work through challenges and difficulties, but I found it always made me feel stuck.

Recently, someone recommended cognitive processing therapy. I will keep it in mind for the future if I have another relapse of PTSD symptoms. It seems intriguing, but hard to find in the area I live. I feel like I would get the most value out of it when my symptoms are active. I haven't looked at it for more than about an hour, so it is difficult for me to say whether it's for me, but I may explore further. I am mentally healthy today so it would be something to keep in my back pocket if I start to struggle again.

Having a creative outlet has been a better option for me. Writing is one of my outlets and I have been involved in a few articles that deal with sexual assault. The amount of power and strength that I have felt just putting my thoughts, memories and feelings in writing has been a big relief. I could feel a pressure lifting as I was getting everything out. For others, it is drawing, poetry or music. I have friends who use pottery as their outlet. As long as it allows for a positive impact, it is worth exploring.

I could be more active. My mental state gets a lift from yoga and I have always felt better after exercise. I was excellent with this for a long time, going to the gym five to six times a week. I let that drop, and have never picked it back up.

For a while, I played ultimate frisbee three or four nights a week, but I lost interest. These days I have gotten more into biking, but even that I do not want to do every day. Finding the balance and combination that works is the key.

When it is nice out, my dog and I do go for walks. Some days they are short, others they are long. We are nice weather walkers, so when the winter comes, we need a bit more of a push to do it. OK...I do; she loves the snow. I am OK with snow but it is the cold I have an issue with.

I have a financial background, so that area is easy for me. I naturally do this.

There are more ways in which I can promote my own version of self-care, but the ones mentioned are where I find I need to focus the most. Finding what works is a process of trial and error.

Chapter 18

Time For Change

*W*hy do I share all of this? Why now? What is the point? The point is that this happened. This is real. You are now connected to someone who went through this. You should be enraged. It isn't something that just happens in the movies, by those with access, in rougher communities, dark alleyways or at gunpoint. It happens in your backyard. It happens here, and it needs to change. I am one of the lucky ones, if you can even call it that. I had the support around me to get through it, to get the help I needed and to heal. It wasn't an easy or quick process. I didn't heal on my timeline. I failed a lot. I lost even more. Almost everyone in my life walked away. People have come into my life and blamed me. That's bullshit. I have been told I must hate men. Not true. I have been told I am too broken. I have been told my issues are too much to handle.

I am far from perfect. While I can now comprehend what a victim feels and goes through after this type of assault, that wasn't always true. I am naïve in many ways and prior to my assault I didn't think about it very much. I didn't appreciate how often we hear about assaults and I definitely did not process them the same way. I used

to be fearless. I would walk home from the bar if it was a nice night. My house was a 30-ish minute walk from downtown and I never felt scared or unsafe. It wasn't always well-lit areas, I had to walk by a cemetery, then a hospital (the one I would later be treated at), and then still a few more blocks before I would be at my door. And I did this alone. Not just once or twice. Sometimes friends would insist on walking home with me. Other times a friend would be staying over so we would walk together, but it was never a thought that crossed our mind. Now that makes my skin crawl. It is sad that we live in a world where we have to question whether or not it is safe to walk home.

I was at another post-Nationals after-party at one of the local bars. We were all having a good time even though we had an early morning flight back out East. Most of our team went back to the hotel pretty early except for two of us. I stayed with a friend on one of the other teams and we left the bar and went back to the hotel to continue celebrating with others who were already there. Another girl on my team disappeared earlier in the night without any of us knowing. My teammates and coaches had a similar thought about me. Oh it's Tori, that girl can handle herself. We don't have to worry about her, she will get back. It is true, I did. I was very aware of the time and I was more than prepared to still be drunk on our early morning flight. (By the way, I do not recommend this. Canada is very large, and flying across it while drunk, and then coming off that into hangover is torture). The other girl wasn't so lucky. She was raped that night. It isn't my story to tell, so I will not go into details or mention names. But I remember hearing about it and not being able to process what I was being told. I believed her and that something bad happened, but linking what I was hearing and attaching that experience to her was difficult. I had never heard things like this happening to someone I knew. It felt like I was being given the wrong information. I saw her as such an innocent girl, and this information went against that. It stole her innocence. No one wanted that.

She reacted vastly different to how I did. She did what many do. She swept it under the rug and never spoke about it again. She went on as if nothing had happened. I saw her at the bar a few weeks later and felt I should look out for her. We happened to be at the same bar, but hadn't gone out together. I was there with some friends from class and my boyfriend at the time. His brother was interested in her that night, but I told him she was off limits.

Her experience and mine are not the only ones I know. Over the years I have had multiple people open up to me about events in their past. I have had to take a stand for a few who didn't feel strong enough to do it themselves. I find it interesting that some of these women who have opened up to me didn't know I had been through similar experiences. They opened up to me because I felt safe to them. I was subbing on an ultimate team with one girl. She was having a really hard time with one of the male player's use of "rape" to describe their past games. She was trying not to shake as she told me how uncomfortable it made her feel. She told me some details about her history without me asking. I told her I understood but she didn't seem to believe me. Then I said, "No really, I've experienced it, too." Those couple of words seemed to bring back her confidence. Knowing there were others made her feel less alone. I dealt with the issue.

We truly don't comprehend the aftermath of these types of assaults. We stop at the rape. We feel sorry for the person for a few moments and talk about how change is needed. But there is a huge ripple effect. I am the one who was raped, but I am not the sole victim. My family, my friends, anyone who interacts with me is impacted. I don't let most people touch me. I still find it very uncomfortable when people who are not on my "OK" list get close to me. I hear things in the media and I can breakdown. I had a really hard time with the #metoo movement. It was also around the anniversary of my rape, and everyone wanted to talk about it. I couldn't get away. I need to get away sometimes.

The outlook of those around me has changed, too. Their feelings are more vivid. Some get really angry. Some defensive. And some feel like they should have done more. My assault brought up stories they had buried. We found out about situations that had been kept secret. Some also had to finally deal with feelings they had tried to drown years before. Hearts were broken.

I never wanted to be an activist. It has never been a desire of mine. I have my opinions and I share them with friends and family, but beyond that I haven't been overly vocal. But if I'm not, who will be? At some point, I had to accept that I am strong enough to do it. I will face a lot of negative feedback and that is difficult to grasp. People will try to tear me down. That is the nature of what we do. When we don't understand or our values and morals are put to question, we get defensive and we attack. I don't believe this is deserved, but I suppose it is something I need to accept. Trolls exist in all aspects of our lives and it is easier now with social media. It is easy to be brave when you don't have to see someone, empathize or sympathize with what they have been through. The whole notion of walking a mile in someone else's shoes is lost.

Chapter 19

National Issues

There are things happening right now in our country, our continent and our world, that are adding to this issue. We should be helping, not hindering and adding to the trauma that any assault survivor goes through. Just this past fall the Ontario Courts ruled that individuals who are accused of sexual assault can use intoxication as a defense. So, intoxication is now in the predator's favour. I realize this is a defense for some other crimes, but it doesn't make any sense. Anyone else thinking "What the Hell?" and scratching their head?

This is ridiculous and wrong. And you know what, if I was a predator, I would damn well be making sure that I took some shots right before forcing my way with someone. How the heck did this get through? You know what ticks me off more about this? This protection for predators was ruled by a woman! That makes it hurt more to me. I feel like my own gender has just put us back 30 years. We have been fighting on all levels to be taken seriously in work and in play. I cannot even start to comprehend the thought process here.

I am so sick and tired of hearing about the damage and irreparable impacts a conviction can have on the predator.

WAKE THE FUCK UP!

Why are we so focused on protecting the predator? Why are we making it easier for them?

We need to focus on the survivor! When is the rest of the criminal code going to catch up? Can I now use alcohol as the defense for hurting my predator? How far can I go? Physical assault? Castration? Murder? Sounds ridiculous, right? I can't think of anyone who would say "It's OK that you murdered your predator, you were drunk. You didn't know what you were doing. You weren't in your right mind." Would you go for that? Didn't think so. Doesn't it sound insane when you spell it out that way? I think so. But this is where we are at.

Sexual assault is not a crime that is often falsely reported. It is already so difficult to come forward. Once you do, there are so many steps to take to have a strong case. We have the statistics: 1 in 4 women and 1 in 6 men. Appalling, and yet we still don't understand where our focus should be. We don't understand how to stop it. We still want to make it as comfortable as possible for predators. That's what they are — let's say it again — predators. I don't care if the predator is 14, 35 or 79, they're still a predator. The thought that assault is OK went through his or her mind. They felt entitled to make sexual advances on their victim. It doesn't matter what their victim is saying or their body is screaming, it is what the predator wants in that moment that matters.

I have been told to be careful about using the age of 14 as an example, but look at what happened at St. Michael's College School only a year ago. A group of six, 14- and 15-year-old boys used a broom to sexually assault another student on the football team. At 14, you know better. These kids are monsters and they should be tried and convicted as such. Yes, they may still be figuring it out, but come on, at 14 you know where brooms do and do not belong. Don't even try to use the excuse that they did not know any better.

We have a crisis around who should and should not be held accountable for these crimes. I could write an entire book chronicling the sexual assault cases in recent years, but where would it end? These are only the high-profile cases, but what about the ones that have gone unreported out of fear? What about the ones where it was too late to do anything about it? What about the ones who were told by authority figures that they were lying — or worse — to blame?

What will it take for us to listen? At what point will we say enough is enough? It is starting, but we still have so many obstacles to overcome that it is hard to even see the light at the end of the tunnel. We have generations of biases and un-learning to do when it comes to how we handle sexual assault. How do we get there? What does that look like?

Take my situation, for example. With our current approach, the second I looked away from my drink makes me at fault. Sounds pretty harsh, but that's how things currently are. For women, our protection against sexual assault is us. No one else. The entire responsibility falls on our shoulders. We hear it over and over again.

- Don't drink too much
- Don't be too open
- Don't let anyone buy you a drink
- Don't look away from your drink
- Don't wear anything that draws attention to you
- Don't wear clothes that "are asking for it"
- Use a buddy system
- Never be alone

- Don't talk to strangers
- Know your surroundings
- Spot the exits
- Stay in well-lit areas

That is it.

We hear rumblings from individuals who are unsatisfied with these options, but we have so far to go in making change. When is the other party responsible?

You would think one of sound mind would recognize that we have an issue. Sexual assault is almost a perfect crime. There is disbelief that it happens, it is very difficult to prove — and worse — when it is proven our courts have a history of being lenient on the predator. If we died, our predators would serve a reasonable sentence (if they were caught that is), but because we are still here to talk about it, somehow that results in taking pity on these individuals.

In recent history we have had the ordeal with Epstein. He had so much power that it took years for anyone to have the courage to speak up. For that period of time they were silenced. Coming forward is brave. I am so proud of these women for their ability to find their voice. For their ability to say enough is enough and demand a change. While I understand that the victims were robbed of the justice they were deserved when Epstein took his own life, I also hope that they feel a bit of relief. Their monster is gone and he went in a shameful and selfish manner. I will not mourn his death and I hope these women do not either.

We can also reflect on the case of Larry Nassar. The destruction and chaos he caused to the innocent girls of USA gymnastics can never be forgiven. He is another individual who took advantage of his power. How did he get away with it for so long? And who else is guilty of assisting in his acts? Children as young as five were his victims. It makes you wonder who you can really trust.

We hear these stories and yet still hear doubts. Still hear that there are those who believe rape is not a thing. That we chose to accuse others of rape or sexual assault for attention. And those, including our judges, who still believe that we need to consider the impact on the convicted.

Let's take a look at the case of Sam Fazio, a Vancouver teen who was raped by another student. Her predator was convicted not only of raping her but also of raping another individual. The judge deemed him unlikely to be a repeat offender. Ummm hello? He *already* is a repeat offender. There are two victims. One plus one equals repeat! Because of this incorrect — and quite frankly outrageous — conclusion he was sentenced to two weeks in a detention centre and the remainder of his time "under supervision." You know what her sentence was? A lifetime of remembering, of fearing what could happen, of panic attacks, of being unable to fully trust another human being, of always wondering how and if she could have done something differently.

Out of curiosity I looked up our criminal code in Canada in regards to sexual assault. This is what I found:

Everyone who commits a sexual assault is guilty of

> *(a) an indictable offence and is liable to imprisonment for a term of not more than 10 years or, if the complainant is under the age of 16 years, to imprisonment for a term of not more than 14 years and to a minimum punishment of imprisonment for a term of one year; or*

(b) an offence punishable on summary conviction and is liable to imprisonment for a term of not more than 18 months or, if the complainant is under the age of 16 years, to imprisonment for a term of not more than two years less a day and to a minimum punishment of imprisonment for a term of six months.[5]

This webpage was recently updated (earlier this month actually), however the law was in place at the time Sam Fazio's rapist was convicted. He would have been 16 at the time he committed this rape, and the criminal code already takes into account his age. Sexual assault is a heinous crime and anyone charged of it should be tried as an adult and not as a youth. However, even though it was already known that her rapist had sexually assaulted another, the judge (who had no criminal law experience), felt that he should be tried under the youth code. So, already the rapist was given the benefit of the doubt.

How about the sentencing of Brock Turner? Although it happened in the US, it was big news in Canada as well. What did he serve? Oh, three months? Hmm…doesn't seem to match the crime if you ask me.

Why the hell are we trying to make sure the predators are looked after and don't pay too much for their crime? Are we forgetting they committed a violent act? It seems that because we are alive and not dead our courts feel they should be let off the hook. It doesn't make any sense. Why is it because they have penises that they shouldn't have to suffer and have their lives ruined too? I am sorry, but they fucking deserve it. Three months? Two weeks? How is that a deterrent for potential rapists? If I was them, it seems like it is worth the risk. I want her, she doesn't want me, well I can force myself on her and the courts will take pity on me. I might have to go to jail for a few months, but ah fuck it, I'll just argue that the way she was dressed made me do it and in no time, I'll be back out in the world. Society will side with me, it always does.

The punishment and repercussions do not fit the crime. I do not understand why we don't see that. I don't understand why this is such a foreign concept. We need to demand more. We need to demand change.

Change is tough and getting to the right people is hard. When I first went through this, my sisters and I teamed up on a solution for some of these issues. I won't go into more details than that, as someday we may come back to it. We actually got as far as getting approved by the National Research Council of Canada's Industrial Research Assistance Program (IRAP) for a grant to explore further. We were assigned a team to work with us, but they couldn't get their heads past the fact that we couldn't guarantee that all rapes would be prevented. We used the example that seat belts were once at this stage, and they don't stop all deaths in collisions. They stop a lot, but they aren't fool proof. I was frustrated and tired of dealing with closed-minded people. Developing something that will solve 100% of rapes is an unattainable target. But stopping one — just one — would be a success. It would be much more effective than that, but when the acceptable target is 100%, you are talking to deaf ears.

I was excited to read *Whatever Gets You Through*, a book by twelve survivors of assault who were strong enough to write about life after assault. They wanted to show how each of their journeys was different. I expected some to be sad and others to show that there is life after assault. I was disappointed. One of the twelve stories was exactly what the back cover led me to believe the book to be. One story was OK, it would get a pass, but was not quite as impactful as it could have been. The rest left a lot to be desired.

Here I am, a survivor of assault, and looking to see how my experiences are similar to and different from others'. I was expecting to hear about the hard times, but also what they have done to help themselves. Instead, some of the essays were simply nonsense. I came away from a couple of them not understanding what I just read or how it was an example of life after assault. I did not expect to hear the details of their assaults, but I found it to just be a "woe is me" type of book. There is absolutely going to be an aspect of that. You can read that here in my own, but what are you doing about it?

It seems like these individuals gave up. They complained about hearing others' stories. They wrote only about how their life is harder, but didn't offer solutions. As victims of assault, our lives are harder than they were before. As child victims, I am sure that life has always been hard. I just didn't take away from their essays that many of them were doing anything to help with the darkness they now face.

It made me nervous that readers of my book will feel the same and I do not want that. I want readers to have more clarity on what survivors go through, but I also want them to identify where they can help. How we can start to change the dialogue. How we can educate ourselves and make small changes that will have big impacts. I know it doesn't happen overnight, but I am hopeful that it *does* happen.

Chapter 20

Who Am I Today?

It's a lot harder to get to know me these days. I don't let everyone in, and I am a bit of an introvert when you initially meet me. I take in my surroundings and the actions of individuals before I decide if I am going to let them in. I'm not always right, it would be a lot easier if I was. It takes a certain type of person to accept me. It isn't that I am a mess, but a lot of people can't handle knowing what happened. I have had friendships that have been really great until they find out. I don't exactly go around telling everyone, but I am also not shy about speaking up against bad behaviour. You have no idea how many people use the word "rape" as a verb. "Oh, that exam raped me." "I'm getting raped by the pressure at work." "He raped me in that game." It's not OK. It triggers me every time, and I have no problem educating the individual on why what they are saying is wrong.

My life was drastically changed due to the decisions others made. My world came crashing down and I had to figure out what that meant for me. It took me a long time to get to a healthy place, and even so there are still times when I can fall back.

Who have I become along the way? Would I say I am a completely different person? No. At the core I am still me, but my view and understanding of the world has significantly changed. I am not as blind to what is going on. Even when I try not to hear it, I do.

I take a different view on issues than I once did. I speak up a little more, but I also listen a bit differently. If you have heard the saying "read between the lines," sometimes you need to listen to what isn't being said, as much as what is.

I am still a determined and stubborn individual. I am kind until I'm given a reason not to be. I do not yell often because I do not like to raise my voice in order to be heard. You will hear me, but you will hear me because my demeanour pulls you in, not because I am the loudest person in the room.

I absorb the emotions and attitudes of those around me. I try to avoid long periods of being around negative energy and individuals. I have learnt the impact they have on how I feel about myself and surroundings.

I am an introvert and an extrovert. For those who like labels, I believe that makes me an ambivert. I recognize that in order to recharge I need to have time alone, but I can also socialize and meet new people when the energy levels are there.

I am fairly easy going, until you cross me. Once you do, I will dismiss you.

I am a chameleon who can change depending on who I am around and what the situation needs. I am not fake, but I know that the energy of a room can change the characteristics that I choose to display.

I'm Not the Only One

I am serious, but I like to laugh. I am strong, but every once in awhile can use a good cry. I love summer and dislike the cold. I like to be active, but I also like to nap.

I am loyal to those who are loyal to me. I will be the shoulder to lean on when the time requests it. I will change my plans if it means making sure you are OK. I will sit with you when everyone else is living life, if that is what you need. I will be there to help you get back on your feet because I know what it feels like to fall.

I am complicated and I am OK with that.

Chapter 21

Be the Change

This was my story, but it is by no means the only story. When you are open to hearing what others have to say you start to recognize the significance of this epidemic. I once thought that sexual assault of any kind was rare. That it wasn't something we needed to worry about. I grouped it in with the boogey man. It was something to be aware of, but not get overly worked up about.

My view has changed.

I hear the stories…and I don't just hear the headline, I hear the trauma, the life long struggle, the search for justice, the pain and the emotional impact. When I hear about a sexual assault and/or rape, I hope the victim is believed, that justice is served and that the courts come out to do their job that day. I hope our judges remember that the victim's entire world was just shattered, and that it is not just that the accused's life will be impacted by a guilty verdict. The sentence has already been issued to the victim, and the guilty should have a more severe one, if it's possible.

Change is a slow process and it takes a time. These issues are not new, but we are living in a time where we are more vocal. I am tired of these issues being swept under the rug, ignored, and twisted to be stories of angry women who want revenge on wealthy men.

I do not know my assailant. I have encountered him on two occasions, once the night he attacked me and once a year later by coincidence. I do not know if he is rich, I assume he is not. I do know he is full of evil. He attacked me, beat me, strangled me and raped me.

I experienced how our current biases have impacted perceptions and influenced victim blaming. My first interaction with someone after my assault was her questioning my character and blaming me. She was trying to talk me down from going any further. Trying to insinuate that I wanted this.

In current events we are seeing change, but not in a good way. We have a US president who openly mocked a sexual assault testimony. We have courts making rulings that make it easier for the accused and then come down with lighter sentences so as to not negatively impact the guilty party's life too much. We have countries where the victim is married off to the rapist, where raped women are disowned, even killed, by their families. We live in a world where a large portion of people will see you as a whore, rather than a victim. They see you as filth and as a liar.

It was easier for those around me to believe me because my assault was visible. While most areas were covered, my arms and neck were bruised. I could show the cuts all down my back. I could show the bruises and cuts on my stomach and my legs. I didn't have to go further and *prove* that the rest of my body was impacted. I didn't need to strip down and show the world every part of me. What they could see was deemed *enough* and gave credibility to my "story."

So, what can we do? How can we help?

Believe Victims

The first thing we can do is believe the victims. Even if you need time to process what you are being told, you need to believe and show them they are not alone. Yes, there will be someone who lies about it. Just like there was the one person who lied about having cancer and held a fundraiser. Those individuals are outliers and need help. They are not a majority. We should not base our entire view off of these few, but currently that is what happens.

Be Aware of Our Words

We need to change our vocabulary. Stop using "rape" as a descriptive word. Educate those around you who do. I hear it most with teens, but not only from that age group. There is no way that a test or a game should be equated to rape.

I hear people joking and laughing that they have drugged someone's drink. It has been said to me on more than one occasion. It has been said by friends/acquaintances to other friends/acquaintances who know what I have been through. This is a trigger for me, and could be for anyone in the room. We need to be aware that our words are powerful. We need to stop this behaviour and elevate people, not bring them down.

Hold Our Judgment

Understand that you cannot judge whether or not this has happened to someone based on what they look like, their interests or who they spend time with. My friend's brother has said to her that sexual assaults do not happen that frequently. His wife has never had an issue, so therefore it must not be something that happens to everyone. He believes that instead it just happens in the "crowd" of people she associates with.

Interestingly enough, we never question whether a boy is telling the truth when we hear in the media about a religious figure assaulting him, yet when it is an adult male, a transgender individual, or female, and the accused is anyone else, we do. Why is this? Do we think religious figures are innately evil and raised to assault little boys? I don't believe this is true, and that seems to be a really big issue if we do.

Look Out for Others

Look out for each other and do not expect the entire burden to fall on the victim. For example, why it is that girls are taught all of the things they shouldn't do, and boys are not corrected for their behaviour? Why are we still stuck on the "boys will be boys" excuse? It is obviously not working.

Education

Sexual education. It is uncomfortable and awkward, I know. The idea of introducing our children to the "private parts" of their bodies and educating them on what is and is not appropriate touching/attention is a hot topic. When is the appropriate time? How young is too young? I get it. BUT — there has to be a way of introducing the topic on a basic level to young children so they know they can listen to their instincts. I know when someone is near me and makes my skin crawl. I know when I feel uncomfortable by someone's choice of words, touch and tone around me. None of that has to do with the act of sex, but it is often sexual in nature. This quote by L.R. Knost sticks with me: "When little people are overwhelmed by big emotions, it's our job to share our calm. Not join their chaos." Wouldn't helping them to understand their emotions and feelings fall under that? We know how to process that, let's help them by giving them the tools to do the same.

Public Awareness

We need a refresher in public education and awareness. "Take Back the Night" walks are not cutting it. I personally dislike them, and they are to raise awareness for those who have been through similar events as me. I am literally the target audience, and it turns me off. I also find it is an event that is easy to ignore. So, if we are only gaining the attention of a select few, it is not effective. We need the attention of the masses. We need more. I am not saying to necessarily get rid of this event because it seems to be invigorating to some individuals, but what about the rest of us? What about those who are not directly impacted or are unaware that someone around them is? We need to evolve on our education. Draw attention to the issue. There should be alarm bells going off due to how many people either don't believe sexual assaults actually happen or don't understand how predominant of an issue it really is.

Encourage Positive Behaviour

We need to teach our children that when someone is not interested in you and have communicated that to you, that they leave them alone. Why do we think this is cute?

"Oh, Suzie is in love with Matthew. She tries to kiss him every day."

"Oh, Bradley is so cute, he really likes Maci and chases her every recess."

We are teaching our children that harassment is OK. What is deemed cute at five, is creepy and unnerving at 20. It is the adult's fault though. At a young age, parents and teachers didn't correct the behaviour, they actually encouraged it. I was the kid who wasn't left alone by a boy in my class and the teachers and his parents thought it was cute. I was angry that no one was listening to me and I just wanted to play with my friends. I didn't want a pretend wedding with him, I didn't want to be chased, and I certainly didn't want him trying to touch me. I was ignored. My feelings were put down. I was "playing hard to get" — well yes, when you are trying to get away that is difficult. But no amount of attention from him was going to change my mind.

It was worse in high school because I was no longer chased around the playground. A boy in my Grade 10 science class who I sat in front of would undo my bra every single class. I asked him nicely to stop and I yelled at him to stop when that didn't work. I asked to be moved to another seat in the class. Want to know my teacher's reaction? He told me to just go out with him and maybe he would stop! I should consider it a form of flattery. Yep — he made sexual harassment OK. I had liked this teacher up until this point, but I lost all respect for him in that moment. He made me feel like this was my fault and that I should just do what the boy wanted.

Guess what? It didn't stop after high school. In first year of university, one of the football players followed me home because he was interested in me. I was staying at a house of upperclassmen on the women's volleyball team. They told me to go into a room and then dealt with him for me.

A guy who knows my sister finds me on every form of social media and constantly says inappropriate things to me. I have had to block and delete him from more than one platform. It doesn't matter how many times I tell him I am not interested; he continues to try. It is at the point that my entire family is aware, and if he comes up to me in public, they all come up with a reason for me to leave the situation. This individual recently reached out to me during the first round of editing of this book. Once again, he was asking to see me, wanting to know what I am up to, if we can get together. He ended his message with "I just thought I would reach out." A couple of years ago I would have just not acknowledged him and hoped he went away. This time I responded:

I wish you wouldn't. Look, I get that you mean well, but I have asked you over and over to leave me alone. I have not had a conversation with you in five years and I really don't feel like I owe you anything. You know my sister, not me. We are not friends, nor do I plan to be friends.

You have made me uncomfortable on more than one occasion. Please just stop messaging me anywhere. No social media, no public hellos, no emails, no texts, no anything.

Pretend you don't know me, because the reality is you don't. I wouldn't have said this years ago...because I didn't feel I could. But I get to live my life and choose who is in it. I have been through more than you know.

My family knows how you bring triggers into my life...to the point they have done their best to shelter me from you and act as a barrier. I get to have space when I ask for it. You do not have the right to continue to try and push your way into my life.

Stop making me be the bad guy and respect my request for space.

That was not an easy message to send. It is harsh, strict and to the point. I am angry that it was necessary and that my boundaries were once again not respected. But this time, I felt I had the power to use my words and stand up for myself. I hate that I felt sorry for him having to receive that message. I hate that I feel like I will be perceived as a bitch for standing up for myself. I have learned, however, that it is OK to voice that my needs come before his wants.

Remember Elliott? Eight months after we stopped dating, he showed up to my house, unannounced, drunk, in the middle of the night. Trying to get me to talk to him. Calling me, texting me and ringing my doorbell, trying to get me to open the door for him. Wanting me to take him back and give him another chance.

None of these scenarios should have happened. Men are not the only ones guilty of this, but my experiences are only with men. We need to teach our children from a young age that this is not OK, so that as they get older, they stop to think. It is engrained in so many that negative attention is better than nothing. That if they try for long enough, the person will cave and come around. This is called harassment. Yes, they should obviously know better, but where is the line? At what age is it no longer OK? Why is there a line at all? Why is it OK until the age of 8, for example, but then not after that? What is the defining factor? And why is it that as a little girl my feelings were not deemed important?

Be Present

We can help those who are struggling by being there for them. Sometimes all we need to do is be there. We do not need to have the right words or advice; silence can be just as effective. Lending your shoulder to cry on can be very effective. I didn't need my friends and family to have all the answers. I didn't need them to tell me it would be OK. I didn't need someone to provide advice or give me a timeline for my healing. Having them be there for me and show me they cared was what I needed. They allowed me to have moments of laughter before the darkness took over. They were patient when

I broke out in tears or had overwhelming emotions that I couldn't explain. That is what I needed. That is what many survivors need.

Healing Takes Time

We need to understand that there is no timeline. There isn't one route that will "fix it." Sometimes survivors just need a bit of assistance in finding the light. For some, it is faith. For others, it is justice, family, friends. Some need to continue on as if nothing happened at all. Some need to stop and grieve the life that has changed forever. They need to allow themselves to feel everything and they will know when they are ready to move forward. We can help those who have experienced these situations move forward with their lives and not get stuck in the anger. In doing so, we need to be patient. There will be ups and downs. There will be baby steps forward and giant steps back. One day survivors will be strong and ready to take on the world, other days their fears will take over.

Speak Up

Finally, those of us who are strong enough can use our voices. We need to tell our stories and share our experiences. Staying silent has not worked and it is no longer an option. We need to learn from our past and make the future better. We need to make it easier for someone else. We need to educate the public on the severity and help to increase awareness of the issue. Together we are stronger. Together we can provide support that others do not have. Together we can be the change.

References

Government of Canada. 2019. "Criminal Code (R.S.C., 1985, c. C-46)." *Justice Laws Website.* May 23. Accessed May 26, 2019. https://laws-lois.justice.gc.ca/eng/acts/c-46/section-271.html.

—. 2018. "Sexual misconduct myths and facts." *Goverment of Canada.* August 10. Accessed May 26, 2019. https://www.canada.ca/en/department-national-defence/services/benefits-military/conflict-misconduct/operation-honour/understand-prevent-respond/supporting-tools-resources/myths-facts.html.

RAINN. 2019. "Victims of Sexual Violence: Statistics." *RAINN.* Accessed May 19, 2019. https://rainn.org/statistics/victims-sexual-violence.

SexAssault.ca. 2014. "Sexual Assault Statistics in Canada." *SexAssault.Ca.* Accessed May 25, 2019. https://www.sexassault.ca/statistics.htm.

Step to Justice. 2018. "Steps to Justice." *What is a conditional or absolute discharge.* Accessed August 25, 2019. https://stepstojustice.ca/questions/criminal-law/what-conditional-or-absolute-discharge.

About the Author

Born and raised in Canada, Tori Hill never intended to be an activist. One horrific night changed all that. Now a proud feminist and promoter of change, in her shocking and hopeful memoir *I'm Not The Only One,* she challenges her readers to advocate for change.

Endnotes

1   SexAssault.ca. 2014."Sexual Assault Statistics in Canada." *SexAssault. Ca.* Accessed May 25, 2019. https://www.sexassault.ca/statistics.htm.

2   Government of Canada. 2018. "Sexual misconduct myths and facts." *Government of Canada.* August 10. Accessed May 25, 2019. https://www.canada.ca/en/department-national-defence/services/benefits-military/conflict-misconduct/operation-honour/understand-prevent-respond/supporting-tools-resources/myths-facts.html.

3   RAINN. 2019. "Victims of Sexual Violence: Statistics," RAINN. Accessed May 19, 2019, https://rainn.org/statistics/victims-sexual-violence.

4   Steps to Justice. 2018. "What is a conditional or absolute discharge" *Steps to Justice.* Accessed August 25, 2019. https://stepstojustice.ca/questions/criminal-law/what-conditional-or-absolute-discharge.

5   Government of Canada. 2019. "Criminal Code (R.S.C., 1985, c. C-46)." *Justice Laws Website.* May 23. Accessed May 26, 2019. https://laws-lois.justice.gc.ca/eng/acts/c-46/section-271.html.

Manufactured by Amazon.ca
Bolton, ON